AF322664

NUMBER YOUR STORIES
And Lead Like a Legend

NUMBER YOUR STORIES
And Lead Like a Legend

MAJ Logan Phillips

This is a work of nonfiction. Nonetheless, some names, identifying details and personal characteristics of the individuals involved have been changed. In addition, certain people who appear in these pages are composites of a number of individuals and their experiences.

The views and ideas expressed in this book are those of the author and do not reflect the official policy of the United States Military Academy, the Department of the Army, the Department of Defense, or the U.S. Government.

First paperback and hardcover editions - November 2023

Paperback ISBN: 979-8-8689-3835-1
Digital ISBN: 979-8-8689-3841-2

Subjects:

PRINTED IN THE UNITED STATES OF AMERICA ON ACID-FREE PAPER

Published by E.P. House
www.ephouse.co

For Dad,
the best storyteller I ever knew.

And, for David and James,
my favorite adventure.

.... TABLE OF CONTENTS

.... STOKE THE FIRE

"If we want to change the world, we have to go back to a time when warriors would gather around a fire and tell stories." – Paulo Coelho

Welcome, welcome. I'm glad you could come; I've been hoping to talk with you for some time and I'm grateful you would reach out. Roll one of those old stumps over here and have a seat with me next to the fire. Before you get too comfortable, grab a frosty beverage of your choosing. Lord knows you've earned it.

Growing up, I loved to sit with my dad and his buddies around a fire and listen to them share old war stories. Even as a child I couldn't help but notice that everyone always seemed a bit livelier when they had a cold drink in their hand. How I loved listening to those stories. There was something about them, ya know? I must have heard those tall tales at least a hundred times each, but every time I listened to them, they seemed to get more interesting. There was something about knowing that my dad and his buddies were really in those situations. A real person, someone I knew and respected, had survived some great ordeal and emerged victorious and wiser. I could see myself in their shoes, learning and growing alongside them.

I've read a lot of books since then, especially after beginning my career in the Army at West Point, nearly two decades ago. Certainly, there has been a fair share of military and leadership focused text. But if I'm being perfectly honest, those classic leadership books almost always strike me as painfully boring. *Where's the action? Where's the fun?* I'd rather sit around a fire like this one with some old dudes any day of the week and listen to them rattle off some gems. But if we're talking books, I prefer a good science-fiction or action-adventure novel. I like to call them "cotton candy" books—no real substance, but super fun to rapidly digest. On the other hand, all that dense military and leadership reading is analogous to eating your vegetables; they aren't much fun, but necessary for your growth. So, throughout the years, wanting to grow up big and strong into a good professional, I'd clean my plate and grit through the often monotonous and bland tomes of essential, but boring material.

Don't get me wrong, all that military reading has undoubtedly helped me to develop throughout my career. And of course, there are exceptions to every rule (I found *Redeployment* by Phil Klay to be especially enjoyable), but for the most part I just do not find those kinds of books tremendously fun to read. Furthermore, I think that I often gain just as much utility out of a well-crafted work of fiction than any high-brow, academic military writing. For example, Orson Scott Card's *Ender's Game* is rife with potent leadership lessons. Other works, such as Isaac Asimov's *I, Robot*, helps you understand the nature of humanity. Even more artistic pieces like poetry and sculptures examine the human experience and express emotion on a deeper level. All these things are critical when understanding the highly complex nature of leadership.

Yet, despite all these great books out there, my most preferred modality for gaining insight into our profession is by talking with people whom I respect. I could sit for hours listening to their stories. Some of the anecdotes are about their personal triumphs, others talk about a time when they faced a moral dilemma. But in all cases, they helped me to better understand the framework for how these mentors became the person they are today. Additionally, I think they are almost always fascinating. There is something special about sharing in the lived experience of a beloved mentor. It's reminiscent of elder tribesman sitting around their own campfires, passing down their wisdom to the younger generation. There's something about the experience that feels primal and almost magical.

This book is an attempt to capture some of that magic. My hope is to bridge the gap between the easily delivered, but often uninteresting teachings of classical military books with the exciting whimsy of in-person storytelling. The tales presented here are a selection of some of the stories I find myself sharing with junior soldiers most often. Though a pale substitute, I have tried to preserve the same narrative style and feel as though we were truly sharing these stories over a couple of drinks. For this reason, I genuinely recommend the consumption of a suitable beverage to accompany any further serious inspection of this book. So, throw another log on and stoke the fire. It's going to be a long but exciting evening as we journey through some of my collected stories.

We'll look at how to create a successful team, looking inward to draw out purpose and analyze the structure of powerful relationships. Once we've successfully joined a winning team, we look backwards to assess our experience with hardship and how this trauma continues to impact our life. Only by letting go and learning from these moments are we able to rise above and leverage our past for future success.

With this baggage no longer weighing us down, we will look at various lessons learned for excelling in a professional military environment. I call them "golden nuggets for success" because these lessons, though priceless, are often hidden below the surface and regularly passed by without deeper inspection. Lastly, we will pause and reflect on our life, learning to respect the journey we are on and number our stories.

···· PART ONE: BUILDING BONDS OF PHILIA

1 ···· STATUES

> *"The purpose of life is not to be happy. It is to be useful, to be honorable, to be compassionate, to have it make some difference that you have lived and lived well."* — Ralph Waldo Emerson

> *"Listen to your mother!"* — Mom

Why are you here? I don't mean in the existential "why are any of us here" kind of way, but why are you here with me right now? What led you to this moment and where are you going?

If you're reading this book, you're likely already considering a life of service and leadership. Chances are, you're looking for purpose and direction, soaking up as much as you can as you plot out your next life course. I believe that you know there is something profound and purposeful out there in the ether, and you are feeling compelled to rise up and find your place in this universe.

There's a Bible verse in the book of Isaiah that says, "Then I heard the voice of the Lord saying, 'Whom shall I send, and who will go for us?' and I said, 'Here am I; send me!'"

I've read that verse over a thousand times before joining the military and long after. There's something about it that continues to resonate with me, as it speaks to an ancient, primal part of my soul. More than likely, you've felt it, too. To us special few, such a call to service beckons us forward, spurring us towards something more. When others stayed silent, we stood up and answered like our friend Isaiah, "Here am I; send me!"

But why?

Could it be that we were born different? Maybe there is something in our DNA, a special "warrior gene" that compels us to serve. Perhaps we grew up playing with enough GI Joe toys and watching enough old war movies that set our course. Certainly, our heritage and upbringing had something to do with it, but I don't think that's quite all of it. I believe a call to serve is within all of us, but few have the opportunity, capability, and willingness to accept the challenge. Understanding and articulating your own specific reasoning and set of circumstances for serving will better root you in your purpose, especially throughout the tough roads ahead.

For me, the difference was statues.

I grew up in a generational military family. My dad was a career Air Force officer who fought both in Vietnam and Operation Desert Storm. My great-uncle served in the 82nd Airborne during WWII. During that time my mom's father piloted a Higgins Boat, which landed on Normandy Beach on D-Day. Our military lineage stretched back for generations as far back as the Roman legion, if you believe our family legends. As a young person, I don't recall ever making a conscious choice to join. It was never a question of *if* I would serve, but rather *how* I would serve.

Later in life, I married another service member. Her parents and grandparents also served. And, though I would never pressure my two children to join the military, it is almost statistically certain that one of my boys will sign up one day. We are a family of warriors, it's in our blood; it's just who we are.

As the son of a pilot, I *knew* that I wanted to join the Air Force. I'm not sure it was ever a conscious decision, but for as long as I can remember I had my sights set on flying the skies like my old man. Toy airplanes and stickers decorated my childhood room. I even had a full pilot's costume, complete with an authentic leather bomber jacket that I wore as a small child that eventually was hung on my bedroom wall. During my junior year of high school my peers began investigating various colleges, but the choice for me was easy. I was going to the Air Force Academy.

Not surprisingly, my parents were ecstatic. Dad called some of his battle buddies from his days in the service and immediately organized a tour of the campus. I had visited once or twice as a tourist, but never had the opportunity to go inside. It was unimaginably beautiful—the architecture, equipment, and pictures of the most hardcore fighter jets at every turn. After receiving an official tour of the campus, my mind was made up. I knew where I was going, or so I thought.

Immediately upon returning home, I filled out and submitted my one and only college application. I even had my senior pictures taken with Air Force Academy memorabilia, which to this day remain hanging on the wall at my parents' house as a cheeky reminder of my adolescent fervor. The punchline is, of course, I did not go into the Air Force. Nevertheless, young me was set in stone; my mind was made up and come hell or high water, I was a Zoomie through and through.

My mom, on the other hand, was less convinced. And against my infinite teenage wisdom, I gave in to her constant pressure to "investigate all the options," and visited the other service academies. It seemed a pointless endeavor, as I was completely confident in my original choice. After all, I was seventeen and basically had figured out all there was to know about life. Still, if it appeased her, I decided it couldn't hurt to just look at the other academies. So instead of partying with my friends during my junior year spring break, I begrudgingly hopped in the car with my family and made the eighteen hours' drive to check out the other services.

To be honest, I am continually baffled by what an ungrateful little shit I was as a teenager. My loving parents took time off work to drive me all the way across the country because they wanted the best for me. And more than likely, I spent the entire time bitching and moaning about not getting to go to some stupid high school party. *God bless them.*

Our first stop was the Naval Academy. I'll be honest, I'm not a big fan of the water, so the idea of spending all my days on a boat was less than exciting. But during our visit I learned that the Naval Academy also graduates cadets into the Marines. I did not really know much about the Marines except they always look badass in movies and their uniforms looked dang good on commercials. Even still, that was enough to pique my interest. They took me around the campus and showed me a few of the classrooms, as well as where some of the boats were docked. They even have an incredible fully connected series of buildings called Bancroft Hall, which is the largest college dormitory in the world. Today, I know they're all a bunch of dirty Squids[1], but I'd be lying if I said that at the time I wasn't impressed.

After we left the Naval Academy, I was still set on the Air Force. But when we visited the United States Military Academy at West Point, I immediately sensed a connection. It felt as though I'd gone back in time and somehow, inexplicably, was watching the founding of our great nation play out before my very eyes. Huge granite structures were ornamented in neat rows of antique cannonry and stood proudly as they overwatched the picturesque Hudson Valley. Everywhere we visited—the mess hall, *the million-dollar view*, even the barracks, I felt like I was walking through history.

---

[1] Just kidding, you know I love my Navy brothers and sisters! Well, except for one night a year at the Army-Navy football game. In that case—beat Navy!

I was impressed by the academic programs and training regimens, the classrooms and labs weren't overcrowded and were well-stocked, and everywhere we walked we saw groups of cadets running or marching in formation. I respected the teaching staff and was excited about the sports programs that West Point offered. There were so many things that resonated with me.

But in the end, what ultimately changed my mind was the statues.

Both the Air Force and Naval Academies are littered with amazing displays of planes and ships. These unspeakably beautiful replicas of technological marvels serve as a testament to American ingenuity and might. But as I walked around West Point, all the statues were of *people*. There was Patton, MacArthur, Washington and Eisenhower—great leaders and warriors. Looking into their marble faces, I realized the Army is about *people*. Yes, we have tanks, guns and bombs, too. But, at the end of the day, *we* are the weapon.

Listen, I have the utmost respect for the other branches of service. Countless men and women have devoted and even sacrificed their lives in the service of our nation while serving in the Air Force, Navy and Marines. My own dad and granddad proudly served within their ranks and, until that point, I had imagined myself among them. But for me, something changed that day.

As we made the long drive home, I sat silently in the back of the car staring off into the night sky, quietly reflecting on the epiphany brought about by those statues. I thought about my childhood and the things I found most intriguing. Though I always said I wanted to be in the Air Force, all my interests were pointing in a different direction. I liked shooting and playing in the mud. I liked to camp and hike. As a child, I never pretended to fly planes but instead liked to charge up a hill to battle imaginary enemies in hand-to-hand combat. But most of all, I liked building and leading strong teams as we worked towards a mission. I might have been using the words "Air Force" to describe what I wanted for the future, but during that car ride home, I realized that I was using the wrong name to describe my desires.

That day, my choice became clear. I wanted to go to West Point.

After returning home I thanked my parents for driving me all around the country, adding a special thanks to my mom for her wisdom to prod me to further investigate all the military academies before making a final decision. It seemed she knew what she was talking about after all. When I broke the news to them about my decision, I wasn't sure how they'd react. After all, my dad had spent his entire career as a pilot; I didn't want him to think I was jumping ship, or in this case, plane. Worried they would be disappointed, I thought it best to just blurt it out, like ripping off a band aid.

"I want to go to West Point!" I blurted out.

I looked to my father, trying to read his expression. But instead of disappointment, he beamed with pride and excitement.

"Finally! We've known you were an Army guy since you were a little kid playing in the mud," he bellowed with a laugh. Growing serious, he put his hand on my shoulder and drew me close, "I'm proud of you for going your own way."

It's been an adventure for sure, an adventure that started long before I was even born. Steeped in a family tradition of service, it made sense to join the military. But my decision to break away from my father's example to join the Army was made while staring into the eyes of those statues. The seeds of that decision, however, were sown only a few years prior, while sitting in my high school's first period typing class (yes, for all you TikToking social media youths, we used to have typing class). Another teacher burst into the room, interrupting the class to turn on the news. The date was September 11, 2001. You know the story.

Like so many of my generation, I stood there as thousands of my fellow Americans perished in the flames as a result of a radical Islamic extremist attack on the Twin Towers and the Pentagon. I'll never forget the image of a man, hopeless and desperate, jumping from the building because he'd rather die in the fall then burn to death in the flames. There I stood, a freshman in high school, powerless to help as we watched thousands more die in the carnage. I might not have realized it at the time, but that was the beginning of my decision to join the Army. I wanted to look those bastards in the eyes when we doled out justice. Somehow dropping a bomb on them from an altitude of several thousand feet just wasn't going to scratch that itch.

It was this mode of thinking that influenced my decisions following my entry into West Point. For the majority of my time as a cadet, I heartily believed I wanted to serve in the infantry. My assumption was that being a hard charging ground-pounder would afford me the greatest opportunity for shooting bad guys in the face. But, after one of my instructors shared his experience as a super high-speed combat engineer, I amended my choice. At the time, it seemed that being an engineer offered all the tactical opportunities I had longed for, while also giving me a chance to leverage my intellectual side. After all, the motto of the engineers is *Essayons!* meaning "let us try." In other words, it doesn't matter how unsolvable the problem, give it to an engineer and they'll get the job done. Plus, they blow stuff up, which seemed pretty awesome.

In a similar manner, I decided I wanted to get assigned to Fort Bragg, NC—home of the 82nd Airborne Division and self-proclaimed, "Center of the Universe." At the first opportunity, I competed for a slot to go to airborne school to become a paratrooper and, as I reasoned, become more marketable to join the airborne community. Indeed, I became a paratrooper and went to Ft. Bragg, but I ended up getting assigned to the 20th Engineer Brigade. At the time I was dismayed, but God has a funny way of giving us what we need, not necessarily what we want.

By following my own path, pursuing the avenues I desire while also making the most out of the hands I've been dealt, it has been a most exciting and rewarding adventure. I have disposed of bombs in the blistering heat. I've built roads and bridges, only to turn around and explosively destroy other roads and bridges. I've jumped out of planes in the dead of night and climbed mountains in the freezing snow. I've led troops in combat and commanded hundreds of trainees with a legion of drill sergeants by my side. The Army certified me in the modern army combative program and later paid for my graduate degrees from Yale University. And most of all, I've raised a family and forged deep and lasting friendships of brotherhood a man can only dream about.

In so many ways, the Army has gifted me enumerable opportunities to grow and succeed in a way I simply could not have attained on my own. Even in the suckiest of times, when faced with the most brutally incompetent and illogical of leadership, I try to remain grateful for the holistic experience the Army has provided.

Just as I chose my own way, you must also choose yours. Whatever route you decide to take through life, you better be sure it is a choice you can abide. It can't be some lukewarm, go-with-the-flow and see what happens nonsense. Declare it boldly to yourself and the world. Speak it into being and own it. If you end up adjusting fire later, so be it. But step into the arena and make a stand. Don't be tempted by such blamelessness.

Aside from God, *you* are the master of your destiny. One way or another, you are the one making the choice. Either you choose to be active in your path selection or you choose to let the world send you where it may. But either way, you have a choice. And if you can stand behind your purpose, if you listen to God's voice and loudly proclaim to the world that *this* is what I want to devote my life towards, you will be powerfully emboldened in your journey.

I love the Army with every fiber of my being. But even still, there are days when this job sucks. Early mornings and late nights, missed birthdays and holidays, deployments and constant moving—it can be challenging. So, if you aren't firmly rooted in why you are here in the first place, it might be too hard. On those hard days, remind yourself of your purpose.

Remember the reason you made the choice to serve and continue to make that choice as you drive onward.

Once you've found your calling and defined your purpose, it's time to move forward. Perhaps you're still struggling with this—don't worry, it will come. Analyze yourself, think about who you are and the gifts you've been given, and above all else listen. It might not come from a burning bush, but I'm as sure about this as I am of anything, God always speaks to us. The difficult part is learning to listen. Maybe you've already heard the calling and are already on the path—if so, awesome! You are off to an amazing start. Heck, most people in their thirties don't even know what they want to be when they grow up, so you're certainly heading in the right direction.

Even still, that's just the beginning. Now comes the work. There's a day-in, day-out grind of lacing up your boots and doing what needs to be done. In either case, whether you're still trying to find yourself or you know precisely where you are headed, you've got to find a place to call home. A place where you are surrounded by those sharing an ethos. I hate to break it to you, but the place where you grew up is not home anymore. That is your parents' home, not yours. Of course, you'll be welcome there, but it won't ever be the same as it was when you were a kid. I'll never forget my first summer coming back after joining the military. I was so excited to catch up with everyone. But it was a bittersweet reunion. Friends remained as the same characters they'd always been, acting out the classic high school dramas in an endless attempt to recapture the passion of that once epic party every weekend. It was fun at first, but the nostalgia wears off quickly. They were all still living in the same place, but I'd moved on and couldn't go back. No doubt, you will experience something similar.

Understand that for you, your peers, and the millions of other lost souls out there, we all need to find a home where we can belong. Every one of us is searching for a place to finally feel like we fit. It's a place where we're surrounded by other like-minded individuals with the same values and purpose. Such a place can be a powerful, life-changing environment if you let it.

Frankly, I never really understood how powerful such an organization could be until years later. I'd seen whispers of this truth throughout my life, but it wasn't until I met a young man at basic training that I began to truly appreciate the impact of finding a home. For this young man with nothing, it made all the difference.

2 ···· WELCOME HOME, PVT BROWN

"Home isn't where you're from, it's where you find light when all grows dark." – Pierce Brown

I once had the privilege of commanding a One Station Unit Training (OSUT) company for combat engineers and bridge crewmembers. Soldiers used to attend Basic Training at one location and travel to another for Advanced Individual Training (AIT), where they would receive training to learn their specific job. But to cut down on the cost of transport—and for several other reasons—the Army created OSUT to combine these together for large military occupational specialties (MOS).

At my OSUT, we took brand new civilians and spent about fifteen weeks transforming them into qualified engineer soldiers.[2] I loved it.

---

[2] Since my time in command, Engineer OSUT has been extended to upwards of twenty-four weeks.

After a few cycles, it was hard not to notice some general personality patterns that regularly seemed to emerge. There were the super high performers, the troublemakers, the entitled my-dad-is-a-colonel types, the *Call of Duty* warriors, and the I-had-nowhere-else-to-go people, just to name a few. And based on these personality patterns, I was able to predict how well each soldier would perform. Until one day, PVT Brown stepped off the bus and arrived at my company. He was an outlier.

PVT Brown was 6'5" and weighed a solid 300 pounds. He wasn't muscular, by any means, but he also wasn't morbidly obese. He was just ginormous and reminded me of Hodor from *Game of Thrones*. Like the television character, PVT Brown seemed to be both dumb and slow. It was like his mind and body were constantly wading through a pool of molasses. There was no spark of life or intensity, just a giant dude blobbing around my training events.

The moment he first stepped off that bus, my eye was immediately drawn to this giant of a man and I couldn't help but notice how out of the ordinary he was. He bumbled off the bus and down the walkway, his four packed duffle bags tucked neatly under massive arms as though they were tiny parcels. As other trainees scurried towards the barracks with drill sergeants in tow, PVT Brown sauntered along aimlessly and ambivalent to the ruckus as though taking a stroll through the park.

Then, walking at a snail's pace, he tripped over his own feet and fell flat on his face, his bags and their contents erupting onto the apron of the building. Again, unperturbed by the now swarm of drill sergeants screaming at him to hurry up, he slowly picked up each individual item and carefully placed it back in his bag.

From a distance, my senior drill sergeant SFC Reid and I observed from our stand as all of this took place. A commander's usual battle buddy would be a First Sergeant, but at the time we did not have one assigned to the company. So, SFC Reid stepped up to be my right-hand-man and holy smokes, was he awesome. To this day, SFC Reid (now SGM Reid) is one of the greatest non-commissioned officers (NCOs) I have ever worked with. Tough as nails, intelligent, calm under fire—and somehow, everything he touches turns to gold. (If there is ever a zombie apocalypse, I want him on my team.) So, as I stood beside this exemplar of a man, watching PVT Brown struggle to walk from the bus to the building successfully, he turned to me with a knowing look.

"Holy shit, sir. Looks like we've got our work cut out for us with this one," he said.

I returned the glance with a nod.

"Holy shit, indeed."

PVT Brown was what we would call a *soup sandwich* or a *can't-get-right* because everything he did was utterly inept. He wasn't malicious. He just could not seem to meet the Army standard … or normal human standards, for that matter. Even basic things, like keeping eye contact or maintaining a conversation seemed vastly beyond his abilities. Moreover, he didn't seem to respond to anything we did.

No amount of motivating encouragement, yelling or pushups appeared to affect his performance. Everyone else would scamper around frantically trying to accomplish whatever tasks we had set forth, while PVT Brown would slowly slog about with his eyes on the ground without showing any kind of work ethic, motivation or emotion.

He was a jellyfish floating alone aimlessly, unaffected by the sea of piranhas around him that were intense, cooperative and lethal.

At every turn, he stood out as the weak link in the chain. On the initial physical assessment after his arrival, he failed to do a single pushup or sit-up and ran a 22-minute mile. It was easily the worst I had ever seen. In time, there seemed little hope he would ever be able to make the necessary improvements to pass. Maybe he realized this early on and resigned himself to failure from the beginning; that would at least explain his lack of effort, but I didn't think that was the case. Typically, when a trainee gave up, we also saw a negative attitude—as though they thought *we* were the problem, and not their subpar performance.

But there was something different about PVT Brown. At the time, we couldn't quite put our finger on it. He never gave attitude or tried to "buck up." Instead, he just existed. He was always the last one lined up for formation, always the lowest performer at each training event, always the slowest, always the weakest, and nothing we did ever had any effect on him. To those nearest to him, it was infuriating. Everyone tried to break through his weirdly impervious emotional state, hoping to inspire greatness, but nothing worked. Perhaps even more frustrating was that we couldn't understand *why* nothing worked.

Throughout all of this, SFC Reid and I watched from afar, giving the drill sergeants space to do their job. At the end of the day, I would talk things out with my drills and bounce ideas back and forth, but my personal interactions with PVT Brown (like all the trainees) were limited. Eventually, things escalated to the point that I needed to become involved. In their growing frustration, a few of the more passionate drills were starting to tiptoe at the bounds of acceptability to rouse any emotional reaction from PVT Brown, either positive or negative. After discussing the situation with SFC Reid, we decided to transfer PVT Brown into a different platoon to provide him a slightly new environment in the hopes he would start to develop.

At that time, we also began to investigate how PVT Brown came to us in the first place. He was such an oddity, and his scores were so incredibly low that we couldn't help but wonder how he made it through the recruiting station. As we reviewed his personal data, it was almost entirely blank—no home of record, no next of kin, no high school transcripts. Nothing.

It was only after we called his initial recruiting station that the full picture began to emerge. PVT Brown had been homeless. Since birth, he grew up in the foster care system and was bounced around from one foster home to another. Now, having worked with some foster parents, I am well-aware that many are selfless, godly people who only want to pour out love on children in need. Unfortunately, this was not the case for PVT Brown. One of these so called "homes" was a place of horrific abuse. He and the other children in this family's care had been beaten, burned with cigarettes, and locked in isolation for days with little to eat.

At the age of fourteen, having survived this daily torture, he ran away to live on the streets. And for over five years he survived by eating out of trashcans, hiding from roving gangs, and sleeping under a bridge. By the time he wandered into the recruiting station, the harshness of his life had left him completely detached from the world. Like a beaten animal he had resigned to suffering. It was all he knew.

This news was both heartbreaking and concerning, to say the least. My mind raced with questions. *How should this affect our leadership approach? Is he capable of becoming a soldier?* His social skills and emotional intelligence were cruelly underdeveloped. The trauma he had experienced was so severe that we were not sure how basic training would provide him the space he needed to heal. He needed therapeutic support instead of a drill sergeant.

In light of this revelation, I struggled to decide on the best course of action. The cold, detached, steely-eyed warrior part of me said to simply cut the guy loose and kick him to the curb. He was dead weight and holding back the rest of the unit. Sacrifice the one for the many. If he wasn't making the grade, he's not worth our time and effort. With limited resources, we could be placing our focus on developing the more capable recruits. We're here to win wars, not provide therapy.

Another part of me swelled with compassion, crying out with love and support, wanting to wrap that young man in a warm hug. He had already survived unspeakable evil at such a young age. I wanted to protect the young child of his past who huddled broken and alone on the streets. The image of my own baby boy flashed before my eyes. What if it had been him? My heart broke for him, and I wanted to make sure nothing bad ever happened to him again.

But yet another, more rational part of me realized that both of these approaches were wrong. One too cold, the other too hot. The correct "baby bear" solution lay somewhere in the middle, a mixture of the two. Like a mother bird watching over her chicks, we needed to continue to nurture and care for this young man as he grew in the confidence and protection of our care, at least for the time being. But one day soon, we'd have to throw him from the nest with all his brothers and sisters.

I just prayed to God he would be able to fly. Ultimately, I made the decision to give him until the end of Red Phase, the first of the three phases of Basic Combat Training. We would give him those weeks as an opportunity to grow and catch up as much as possible. We also made sure the chaplain and other physical and mental health resources were made available, if he wanted them. But at the end of Red Phase, if he continued to show no improvement, we would have to evaluate him for recycle (starting over with a different company) or withdrawal. It seemed to be the most compassionate solution possible, while also being good stewards of the Army's time and resources.

Secretly, though, I kept PVT Brown in my daily prayers. I silently cheered him on as I watched the training events. Whenever he would pass by, I'd shoot him a quick word of inspiration.

Finally, the end of Red Phase loomed around the corner. In truth, despite my silent hopes, PVT Brown had not progressed. It seemed almost inevitable that we would either have to recycle him or drop him from BCT completely if he showed no improvement. Moreover, only one training event remained—rappelling off a 40-foot tower.

Easily my favorite Red Phase activity, the tower stretched high into the sky above most of the surrounding foliage. A small rectangular platform perched atop four telephone poles which seemed to sway ever so slightly in the wind. On the back, a rickety old ladder stretched to the top for trainees to climb up. The front side was covered, wooden slats nailed together to create a wall for trainees to place their feet as they rappel down. Long ago someone had sprayed the wall with textured paint in an attempt to give people a better grip, but we always had one or two who would slip and slam face first into the wall.

Besides being an opportunity to learn a useful skill, it was the first time that basic trainees face their fears in a semi-dangerous situation. Obviously, there are significant rehearsals and safety protocols put in place that make it nearly impossible for anything too terrible to happen. But no matter how small, the chance of sudden and painful death still existed.

At the base of the tower, someone had strewn comically ineffective rubber chips to dampen a fall. But everyone knew, if you fell from that tower without being hooked up, you were a goner! I've seen even the most confident, hard-ass trainees turn into a blubbering pile of jelly as they looked over the edge.

My first time rappelling was at West Point. They've since built a tower, but we used to rappel down a sheer cliff. That first time I made a grave mistake and looked down. Staring into the abyss, the cliff seemed to stretch on forever. My heart raced but I took a breath, swallowed my fear, and stepped backwards off the ledge.

The whole way down I was careful to keep my eyes on the cliff face in front of me. But once I reached the bottom I exclaimed, "that was awesome!" and asked to go again, never admitting my fear aloud. Now, having done it hundreds of times, it has become a routine activity that barely gets my blood pumping. As the OSUT commander, it gave me satisfaction to watch new folks battle and conquer that same fear. I looked towards PVT Brown and wondered with anticipation how he would handle his fear.

Again, I said a quick prayer and moved towards the inspection area. Prior to going off the tower, every trainee must use a strand of rope to tie a harness known as a swiss seat. Once their swiss seat is tied off, we inspected it several times to ensure everything was up to standard so they wouldn't plummet to their death. No pressure. As the drill sergeants and I made our way through the formation scrutinizing everyone and making on-the-spot corrections, I came upon PVT Brown. He stood there, rope still in hand, staring blankly into space.

"What's going on here, PVT Brown?" I prodded. "Let's get a move on, we don't have all day. You got this!"

We locked eyes.

It was the first time he had made eye contact with anyone. His were bloodshot and focused, like he was mustering every ounce of energy to break through miles of emotional walls built over his lifetime. His face was tense, as though the very act of speaking caused him pain.

"How do you do it, sir?" he whispered, carefully pushing out each word. "How do you have so much confidence?"

I knew he wasn't asking about the tower. It was as though the weight of everything he had faced in life, from being an abandoned and abused child to failing to meet the demands of basic training, had suddenly come crashing down. This behemoth of a man stood before me, utterly wrecked and silently crying out for support. For the first time since stepping off the bus, he let himself be vulnerable enough to make a connection with another person.

"You've got to have faith in yourself," I answered. "You have to tell yourself that you can accomplish anything. Look how far you've come after all that you've endured. Surely you can do this! Have faith in your training. The Army developed a series of rigorous events to ensure you are prepared for exactly this situation. Think of all the thousands of people who came before you. They weren't any different than you. If they can do it, you can as well."

Then, I softened my voice.

"But if all else fails, have faith in us. We have spent years preparing to get you where you need to be. We are your brothers and sisters. We are a family and we won't let you down."

After a moment of silence, he looked up with tears in his eyes.

"I … I've never had a family," he choked.

That small statement, filled with a lifetime of pain and suffering was almost more than I could bear. I scrambled to think of the right words but before I could formulate a response, my senior drill rushed over. SFC Reid, the toughest man I've ever known, put his hand on PVT Brown's shoulder and looked him in the eyes with earnestness.

"You have a family now."

That was it. That was everything. Those five words changed this young man's world. In an instant, something washed over PVT Brown and he became transformed. Without a word, he flawlessly tied his harness, climbed the tower, and executed the repel without hesitation. After that day, PVT Brown became a completely different person, it was like a switch had flipped in his brain. At every training event and PT session he was completely devoted to the task, and spent his free time practicing and improving, because he was utterly devoted to the Army.

To his family.

Like PVT Brown, we all need to feel like we belong.

Deep within us, there is a primal yearning to be a part of a pack. We are all searching for that place where we feel supported and loved, where someone cares enough about us to hold us accountable and lift us up when we stumble. We're looking for that place that, if something goes wrong, we can take refuge in our time of need. We're all hoping for a brother and sisterhood surrounded by people who have our backs. We all need a family to survive and to flourish.

Maybe you've been fortunate. Perhaps you're like me and were blessed with two amazing parents, raised in the love of God. You've never been hungry or abused; you've always been sheltered and safe. Or maybe you're more like PVT Brown, having overcome tremendous adversity, alone and afraid in a harsh world.

Whatever the case, I guarantee that some, if not most, of those you will lead are aching for a sense of belonging. Without a place to call home, we are lost—wanderers searching for a place to lay our head. You cannot have a successful team unless people believe that they belong. For any leader, this must be a major priority and shouldn't be understated. But to truly excel, to rise above the bare minimum of success and push towards greatness, you need something more.

It isn't enough to just fit in, people need to believe they've earned their place on a winning team. Provide that team. Provide them that family; they are your brothers and sisters. Everything you do must be done out of a deep sense of caring for their well-being. You train hard because you want them to be prepared for the harshness of combat. You provide discipline because you care enough to correct them when they are wrong. You stand up for them when they need rest or support.

And just like a real family, you will mess up. You'll be too hard or too soft. You'll stay silent when you should have spoken up or say something when you should have patiently listened. But if you genuinely care about your soldier's well-being, that love will always shine through.

More than anything else you can do as a leader, the most important thing you can do is *care*. Your soldiers will see it and respond tenfold. There will still be issues and squabbles and infuriating chicanery. But when it counts the most, they'll be there for their family.

The story of PVT Brown always makes me smile. It fills me with tremendous joy to know that I played a small part in helping that young man find a home, which is something all of us deserve. PVT Brown never became an all-star. He never ran the fastest or did the most pushups. He never scored the highest on a test or had the sharpest uniform. But he did become the most committed soldier I have ever met.

Every day he improved, and at the end of those fifteen weeks he walked across the graduation stage with his head high—a proud member of the Army family.

3 ···· YOU CAN'T CARRY MY STONE

"Give me enough ribbons to place on the tunics of my Soldiers and I can conquer the world." – Napoleon Bonaparte

Like most engineer officers, my first real job in the Army was as a Platoon Leader (PL). *Unlike* most officers, I had the opportunity to take charge of a platoon that did not actually exist prior to my arrival. The battalion that we fell under was preparing to return from a deployment in Iraq while simultaneously activating several numbered line-companies. Basically, this meant that for several weeks my "platoon" consisted of a single person … me. In fact, though not pertinent to this story, I was the only officer physically present at the company for quite some time. As soldiers finally began to return from some much-deserved redeployment leave, the platoon started to grow and two important facts emerged from this unusual situation.

First, almost none of the soldiers had worked together previously. Normally, a PL falls in on a pre-established organization that has a history together. They know each other's habits—delegating training responsibilities, coordinating each other's training plans, or identifying subject matter experts for various activities and, for the most part, they already work together as a well-oiled machine. A PL can, and should, take the time to get to know the lay of the land before they attempt to effect change. In part, it's to gain the trust of the unit before you bust in and start changing stuff around. But it's also about respect. Almost certainly, those capable leaders established each process for a reason. If you show up on day one and start changing everything without duly assessing how everything fits together, not only will you break a bunch of systems you didn't even know were there, but you'll also piss off all the people who've spent years crafting the organization.

This process of transitioning into the leadership role of a unit is often explained using the analogy of swapping drivers in a moving car: as the old driver releases the wheel, the new driver gently takes hold and makes only slight adjustments at first to avoid veering off the road. You don't just kick the other guy out the door and start shaking the wheel around like a crazy man. My experience was neither of these situations. Without a departing leader to trade places with—or unit for that matter—it was like trying to drive and build a car at the same time.

Second, for a significant amount of time, I did not have a Platoon Sergeant (PSG). PSGs are the senior most enlisted soldier in the platoon. In addition to being the head NCO for the platoon, they also advise and mentor young platoon leaders. For good reason, NCOs are often referred to as the "backbone of the Army." One of the wisest decisions made by the Army is to pair every officer in a leadership position with a seasoned NCO. At all levels, these NCO counterparts provide officers with guidance, experience, and an essential link to the junior enlisted. PSGs are especially important since their PL has almost no experience. Like a set of bumpers on a bowling lane, a good PSG can help young officers to keep moving in the right direction. The significance of their mentorship cannot be understated. Unfortunately, in the beginning, I did not have a PSG. And holy smokes, I was racking up those gutter balls!

As the weeks progressed, things began to smooth out as my platoon fell into a battle rhythm. This was okay, but I wasn't satisfied. Something still felt off. Sure, we were accomplishing tasks and trudging through the day-to-day minutia—inventories, cleaning weapons, executing training—but there was no sense of real unity.

This became abundantly clear following our first battalion run. In the early morning, a blistering summer sun beamed down on the sandy, asphalt jungle of Ft. Bragg, NC. Over one thousand paratroopers, dripping with sweat, ran the final block of the battalion's first four-mile run since returning from post-deployment leave. Over the roaring sound of warriors shouting cadence, you could hear the pounding *clap clap clap* as their feet hit the ground in perfect unison. There was something both awe-inspiring and ominous about the whole affair, as if at any moment they could change course, charge into the surrounding neighborhoods and take them over. It was both terrible and spectacular.

This was my first time as part of such a large military event. As I ran, surrounded by a mass of soldiers, I looked around and couldn't help but swell with pride as I imagined what it must look like from the outside. Everyone barked cadence and ran in lockstep with each other like something out of the movies, and I got to be a part of it. But the more I surveyed, the more I realized that my platoon, a small handful of soldiers in a sea of similarly dressed warriors, was different. While the others shouted out the songs, whooping and hollering, my team mumbled the words. While others smiled and clapped each other on the back in celebration, my platoon remained subdued and dispassionate. As we finished the run, the battalion commander and sergeant major provided motivational words and then released everyone to their individual company command teams. In turn, the company command teams released their troops over to platoon leadership. Trying to be as energetic and impassioned as possible, I brought the team around for a classic football-style breakdown.

"Great work, team!" I shouted. "Put your hands in. Second Platoon, on three. One … two … three!"

Some of the group gave a dispassionate "second platoon." Others mumbled noises barely above a whisper. I'm pretty sure I even heard someone, either being silly or cynical (perhaps both), shout "stinky deuce!" It was pathetic. I watched as they walked off in small groups heading in different directions. There was no unity. As they left, I could see other platoons breaking down, but in a manner I was more accustomed. From a distance I saw a fellow LT leading his unit in their platoon chant.

"Who are we?" he shouted.

"Wolfpack!" the platoon responded.

"Who are we?" he shouted again, even louder.

Again, they echoed, "Wolfpack!" raising their voices to match his. The whole group started to sway back and forth, huddled in a big circle with their hands on each other's backs.

For the last time, he screamed at the top of his lungs, spitting foaming out the side of his mouth, *"Who are we?"*

This time, in crisp unison, the entire group flung their faces to the sky and howled, *"Aaaaaahooooo!"*

It was more animalistic and fiercer than any pack of real wolves I've ever heard. And holy shit, was it cool. But who were *we*? What was my platoon? We certainly weren't the mighty Wolfpack, that was for sure! We were just "Second Platoon," which I had just realized was super lame. We needed a name, an identity. Up until this point, we were simply a collection of individuals and had not truly become a team. A name gives you something to rally around. It gives you pride and can unite the organization. A PSG would have fixed this on day one, but like I said, it was just me—the rookie LT.

That next Monday, I got to work. Immediately after formation, I rallied all my squad leaders to explain my revelation. They unanimously agreed, some even surprised I hadn't realized the issue sooner. After a short, friendly bout of gently deriding the dumb new LT, we began brainstorming ideas. People threw out the usual names—Bandits, Spartans, War Pigs (that one was new)—but nothing seemed to fit. Eventually, after several minutes of spitballing, I noticed the youngest of the squad leaders looked like he wanted to say something. He kept leaning forward like he was about to speak, but then sitting back in his chair, probably afraid to speak up.

"SGT Cook, you got any ideas?" I nodded towards him.

Everyone turned to look at SGT Cook. For a moment he looked like a deer in headlights, but he quickly regained his composure.

"What about the *Gravediggers*?"

The moment he spoke, everyone knew it was the clear winner. It seemed to convey an appropriate mix of construction capability with a dash of gratuitous violence. Needless to say, it was a big hit.

The next morning, I eagerly brought the platoon together after formation to announce the news. Man, I must have run through that talk at least a hundred times in my head the night prior. For almost the entire time I was at the academy, we were bombarded with the importance of properly interacting with our future platoons. *How are you going to introduce yourself to your NCOs? How will you impart your vision? How are you going to leverage the five types of power to establish your leadership presence?* And anytime we made a mistake as cadets, we were repeatedly assured that such behavior in the future would surely lead to the immediate death of our subordinates. The stakes were high, and I wasn't about to mess it up. But with this kick-ass name, we were going to have the most cohesive, motivated fighting force the world had ever seen.

However, as I stood in front of my team to announce our new unit name, folks were decidedly less excited than they'd been in my mind all the times I'd rehearsed. Sure, they thought it was a good name, some even gave a mildly interested, "oh, cool," but that was the extent of their excitement. No one cheered. No one rallied. No one carried me off on their shoulders. They all just carried on with their day. It was underwhelming to say the least and, if I'm honest, I was both disappointed that it wasn't the huge success I had thought it would be. Negative thoughts loomed in the back of my mind for the better part of the day until, as we were wrapping up training for the day, I overheard SGT Cook talking to his squad.

"All right, Gravediggers," he shouted. "Form up on me."

Something about the way the soldiers rallied around their squad leader, a newfound hustle in their step, stood out. Maybe it was working after all. While this was certainly a step in the right direction, it wasn't enough. Something was still missing. My next revelation came during a talk with my father-in-law, a sergeant major at the time. His wisdom pierced through the darkness like a bolt of lightning to shine down on the situation.

"Sounds like you're missing a soul," he said. "Anyone can be in an organization. That's just the place where you do your job. But to be on a real team, to feel a part of something truly special, you have to feel like you earned your place."

His words rolled around in my head that night as I lay in bed thinking through how his message applied to my situation. Like the turning of a key, something clicked in my mind, and I knew the way ahead. I jumped out of bed, threw on my bathrobe and, grabbing a flashlight, ran into my backyard. No doubt had my neighbors seen me, they must have thought I was certifiable. But sometimes you have an idea that just can't wait. Shining the light through the tall flowers, I finally found what I was looking for—a large, smooth stone.

Just what we need! I thought to myself.

Every Wednesday at Ft. Bragg is known as Sergeant's Time Training (STT). Like the name suggests, this is a designated time for squad leaders to train their squads on whatever tasks they see fit. It is an excellent opportunity for the squad leaders to share their knowledge and expertise with the junior enlisted while also getting some reps on developing a training plan. It's also an incredible opportunity for young NCOs to get valuable leadership experience as they try out new approaches for developing their team. Personally, I'm a huge fan. But for this particular situation, the important aspect for me was that every STT began with a platoon ruck march.

It is customary for the PL to say a few words following each ruck march, not a long speech or anything, just an opportunity to put out notes to the team before everyone breaks away for the day. But this week, I had something extra planned. As we dropped our rucks and began to stretch out, I revealed the smooth, basketball-sized stone I had been carrying in my pack. The standard load for a ruck is at least 35 pounds, but this damned thing easily weighed 60 pounds by itself.

"Alright Gravediggers, this is our new mascot, the 'Gravestone,'" I proclaimed as I unveiled the miniature boulder. "She will accompany us on every ruck march from now on. However, she's mine! No one is allowed to carry her except for me. Is that understood?"

Of course, with the exception of a few strange looks, no one objected. Why on earth would anyone want to carry that giant rock? The following week, I continued the charade in a similar manner.

"All right team, excellent job out there today. The Gravestone and I are proud of your hard work," I started, giving everyone an earnest look of approval. Then, my expression grew stern.

"However," I continued firmly. "I've been getting a lot of requests to carry the stone. The Gravestone and I are flattered, but like I said before, *no one* is allowed to carry her but me."

I put special emphasis on the words *no one* to really drive the point home. This time, people started to mutter to each other. There were a few chuckles. After all, it was pretty outrageous. But for the most part, people were curious.

"Who asked to carry the stone?"

"Did you? I sure didn't."

"Why would anyone want to do that?"

"You couldn't pay me to carry that damned thing!"

On and on it went. Internally I allowed myself a sardonic smile of satisfaction. Of course, no one had actually asked to shoulder the load, but this was all a part of my cheeky little plan. By the third week, I started to feign annoyance.

"Seriously team, I'm getting a little tired of all the requests to take the stone. I've told you several times, but people keep asking. I'm going to say this once more. *No one* is allowed to carry the stone except for me!"

There was an absolute frenzy. For the rest of the week, all anyone could talk about was the stone. Then, as we formed up for the next march, I called up one of my high-performing soldiers to the front of the formation. All the pieces were in place, and it was finally time to have the plan come to fruition.

"Before we start today's march," I began, "I want to reward the efforts of one of our teammates. Against my better judgment, I am going to allow him the *honor* of carrying the Gravestone, if he chooses."

You would have thought I had just gifted him a brand-new car. With excitement, he graciously scooped up the stone and added it to his pack. There was a subtle, almost imperceptive pause as he attempted to hoist his ruck from the ground, only to be surprised by its newfound heft. But not wanting to look weak, he marshaled his strength and flung the pack over his head and onto his back in a classic cool guy maneuver. You could see his squad-mates give him a nod of approval as we moved to the front of formation to begin the long five-mile march.

At the culmination of the journey, as we formed up to release, I called the soldier to the front of the formation. He promptly scurried to the front, perhaps a bit slower than when we had started, and stood proudly at attention. As he stood, I gave a quick talk about how proud I was of his dedication, his hard work, and his resolve. These were precisely the qualities of a real Gravedigger. To finish, I informed the group that for his efforts, I would allow this soldier to sign the Gravestone. With a flourish, I withdrew a shining metallic paint pen I had concealed within my pocket. This was it. This is what we were missing before.

Grinning ear-to-ear, the soldier started energetically shaking my hand and saying thank you, like he had just won an Oscar. The entire platoon peered on in silence, almost holding their breath as they watched him gracefully pen out his signature. Then, as he clicked the cap of the pen back into place, something erupted within the group. People started cheering and clapping him on the back. Everyone was congratulating and giving high-fives as they made their way to get a closer look at the Gravestone and admire the silver signature that shined in the morning sun.

That was it. That was all it took.

Before long, people were almost fighting for the opportunity to carry the Gravestone. Every week I would bestow the honor onto a new recipient. They would hustle up to the front and take her as far as they could. If the burden became too great, we would rally around them to motivate them to the finish line, providing help where needed. Before long, she had made her way to everyone on the team. I remember looking down with pride at the list of all the shiny silver names side by side on the big stone.

After a short time, the Gravestone became a fixture of our platoon. She came with us everywhere, not just on ruck marches. She was brought to training sites, the motor pool, and even to the field. Heck, one of the guys added a bowtie and brought her to the battalion ball. She was a part of the team. She was a rite of passage, a symbol of our shared brother and sisterhood in overcoming hardship. When new soldiers arrived at the unit, they would carry the stone and then sign as a *real* Gravedigger, as their brothers and sisters cheered and welcomed them into the family.

In general, I find that we all want to feel like part of something special. We want the feeling of pride and accomplishment that comes with taking on a difficult task that few others even dare to try. Sure, we like to gripe and complain in the moment, but at the end of the day we—especially soldiers—crave a good challenge. Because with each challenge comes new opportunities to be successful. We want to be proud of the people in our group. We want to believe that our squad is better than other squads; that our platoon is better than other platoons; that the Army is better than other branches. We want to be on the winning team.

You have an amazing opportunity to create something special. Being a leader is not about telling people what to do; it's about creating an environment. Your NCOs are experts at getting stuff done. Yes, you need to be competent. Yes, you need to give them purpose, direction, and motivation and check up to make sure things are going to plan. But 95 percent of the time, they've got it covered. However, the only one in the platoon who is thinking about the environment is you. Don't let that ball drop.

It is not enough to be on a team. Undoubtedly, feeling accepted is important, but it is not enough. To feel truly exceptional, you need to earn your place. You genuinely need to give people the opportunity to meet a challenge. No amount of lip-service will do. It doesn't matter how much you say something is true. If the emperor isn't wearing any clothes, deep down everyone knows. You've got to set a standard and then hold people accountable. It can be challenging because, intrinsic to this methodology, it means that not everyone will rise to the challenge. It is incumbent upon you, as the leader, to both maintain your standards, but also help those who are struggling to rise up. Help them to be stronger, motivate them to be better. Educate and train them to be more proficient as they strive towards greatness. Each day, earn your place as you build a winning team.

But what *is* a winning team? What do they act like? What do they do? Well for one thing, they have a kickass name and train harder than everybody else. I followed my gut and it paid off. Finally, we had become a team. Yes, of course, this was a pretty wild idea and there was a plethora of other experiences that could have helped to strengthen our bond. But in the end, the thing that elevated us from a unit to a family was the weight of a cold hunk of stone.

4 ···· HORNED FROG HILL

"Success is not final, failure is not fatal: it is the courage to continue that counts." – Sir Winston Churchill

Building a sense of belonging and pride in your organization is challenging. It takes focus and regular engagement; it's not something that just happens by accident. But these are just two facets of an even larger, more important objective—developing a positive culture. In my opinion, it is quite literally the most important thing you will do as a leader and deserves serious thought and attention. My military experience is rife with examples of both good and bad leaders, some gracefully steering their team in a positive direction, while others close their eyes and remove their hands from the wheel as they drift off the road. Heck, I've known some bad leaders who seemed like they were actively steering us into a ditch! There are a ton of military examples to observe and learn from. But for me, my first understanding of how culture impacts accomplishment came at a young age during youth football.

We had just started the third quarter of the last game for the youth football season when the officials decided to cancel the rest of the game. The score was a crushing 0-42, but that wasn't even the most embarrassing part. The officials already had to quash two fights between parents in the stands. Now, an additional altercation was breaking out between our head coach, Coach Barry, and one of the referees. By the time the police arrived, all hell had broken loose. Like Napoleon leading a charge into battle, Coach Barry rushed the field with a few of his most loyal parents and players in tow. The last thing I remember, as my parents hurried me away from the field, was looking back to see Coach Barry screaming obscenities while being carted away in handcuffs. That was the last time I ever saw him.

I was nine.

My parents quickly ushered me into the car, hoping to get as far away from the craziness as fast as possible. No doubt both were thinking the same thing—that was the *last* time any of our family would step foot on that field. But as the door slammed shut on our car, I immediately began pleading with my parents to continue to let me play football. Even though I was only in third grade, I understood that the coach's behavior was beyond unacceptable and tangentially jeopardized my hopes of playing ball. He had always been somewhat of a buffoon—screaming at children, cursing at the refs, and even throwing his playbook to the ground when things didn't go his way. He must have broken a new clipboard during every game. Obviously, I knew that stuff was unacceptable, but … I really wanted to play.

Several parents had complained about Coach Barry prior to this final tirade, and he had received multiple "reprimands," but these were just an administrative slap on the wrist. Comprised of his longtime friends and drinking buddies, the league's leadership refused to take any real action against Coach Barry. Nor would they entertain proposals to have him replaced. The guy didn't even have a kid in the league and hadn't for some time. Nevertheless, hoping to live out his dream of being the next Lombardi, he staked out his claim with our team. So, as the only football program in the area, families were forced to choose between putting up with Coach Barry's antics, driving a half hour to play on a different team, or forsaking junior football entirely. Faced with these options, parents begrudgingly elected to turn a blind eye to Coach's shortcomings, chalking them up as part of a figurative price of admission.

I didn't even know why Coach Barry was always so upset. A small, wiry man with a somber mustachioed face, he seemed perpetually angry at the world. In my youth, I didn't have a full understanding of the issue, only that he was always on the cusp of flying off into a needless tirade for the slightest misstep. As an adult, however, I've seen enough similarly tempered men to have a fuller appreciation. He was one of those lost souls whose life never became what he thought it should. He felt owed something, like he had been promised greatness, but it never came. He never got that dream job, he never moved into the huge house with the white picket fence and the sports car in the driveway, and never made it to the big show … but he *could* have!

Oh, you bet he could have, and don't you dare say otherwise. But there was a disabling injury, his coach didn't give him a fair shake, or some other cruel twist of fate let the golden ring slip past his fingers. It's always like that with guys like him. So trapped in the past, feeling like he had so much more left on the field, he was stuck on an endless and impossible cycle. He was forever trying desperately to vicariously change his past through youth, followed by an intense anger when unable to do so.

There appeared to be some major disconnect between what he *thought* should be going on and reality. It was like he had forgotten he was overseeing a third grade little league team and instead expected us to be prepping for the Super Bowl. It never once occurred to him that maybe he wasn't that good of a coach. The thought was absurd; it was us damned no-talent kids that were the problem! Every loss utterly infuriated him as a personal slight.

These frustrations were not in the normal competitive spirit sort of way, but it enraged him beyond measure. If you missed a block, or dropped a ball, or didn't make a tackle, it wasn't because you made a mistake. It was because you were a deficient human being. In fact, he would regularly mock the less athletic kids on the team; always making sure to be just out of earshot of the parents. It wasn't long before other children on the team would join in the fun, taunting the second-string kids for their inadequacies. Negativity and hatred are infectious, especially in young boys finding their way through the wilderness of adolescence. I remember being in constant fear that one day, I would fail to live up to his expectations and incur his wrath and ridicule.

To Coach Barry, winning was the only thing that mattered. You were either a winner or a loser—there was no in-between. The problem was that we lost, *a lot*. In fact, I don't think we won a single game in the two years I played on his team. The more we lost, the angrier he would get. Strangely, he never seemed to take on any of the blame; it was always someone else's fault. The refs were charlatans, the other team was a bunch of cheats, and we—the kids on his team—were worthless. Again, having dealt with people like this more times than I would like, I now understand that a big part of this single-mindedness on score was due to his own feelings of inadequacy. Deep down, he felt like a loser. So, to prove to everyone, most of all himself, that he was *not* a loser, it was imperative that we won. But again, that didn't happen very often.

Unsurprisingly, following the *incident* and his subsequent arrest, the courts permanently barred Coach Barry from working with children. The league had no choice but to either drop the program or have him replaced. However, in solidarity with their fearless leader, none of the assistant coaches would agree to stay on with the team. In fact, some of the loyal families refused to return without their precious Coach Barry at the helm.

It baffled me, even then, why people would remain loyal to such a terribly behaved man. But to them, still blinded by the patina of shared high school glory, Coach Barry represented a voice deep within. He was the embodiment of their frustrations with life. He was a working man's middle finger to the establishment. His callous, grotesque manner was a spit in the eye of all those hoity-toity rich teams with their fancy new gear and turf fields.

As an adult looking back, I can understand those frustrations. I've enjoyed rallying behind someone who finally has the guts to stand up and say what we've all been thinking. Maybe Coach Barry was genuinely the renegade leader they made him out to be, the reincarnation of Bruce Springsteen, rocking out for the little guy. But holy smokes, that man was a *terrible* football coach and had no business anywhere near the game. Genuinely, from the bottom of my heart, I hope Coach Barry found what he was looking for. I hope that emptiness and pain that had so utterly consumed his life was finally eased, and he became whole. But thank goodness it wasn't by coaching little league football. Him leaving the team fundamentally changed the culture of our organization and had one of the most profound impacts on the course of my young athletic life.

Amongst the families that stayed, there was a lot of discussion about the future of the program. If we could not find a replacement by the start of summer, the team would not be allowed to participate in the next season. Luckily, in the eleventh hour, an older brother of one of the boys on the team offered to step up.

The new guy, Coach Hall, was the polar opposite of Coach Barry and was a genuinely good role model for us as young men. In truth, he couldn't have been more than twenty years of age, but in my youthful mind, he was a towering figure, tall and muscular, every bit the picture of athleticism and excellence. He came across as both calm and assertive, almost fatherly. Coach Hall's way of doing things was different, very different. During our first practice, if you can even call it that, we never touched a ball. Instead, he spent almost the entire time talking with the team, as well as the parents, about his vision and expectations for the program.

"I know there have been issues in the past," he began. "But that is no longer who we are. That is not our team."

The first order of business was defining our team values. He went around the group, calling on us to share what we felt like were the most important characteristics of a good team. Then, with these values as a backdrop, we took turns suggesting new team names that aligned with the values we had just set forth.

After deliberating, we decided on the name *Horned Frogs*. I thought it was a good name. Horned frogs are big and tough, at least as far as amphibians are concerned. They survive in the rain and the mud, determined and focused. Plus, they can snatch flies out of the air with their tongues, which was pretty freaking awesome to us boys. With the team newly re-named, Coach took us to a new spot to practice, staking a claim on the land. It was a steep hill a short distance from our usual practice field, past the back of the end zone. The hill was about twenty yards long and at a fairly steep pitch. We'd only been here a few times when Coach Barry had made us do sprints as punishment for being losers. Coach Hall, on the other hand, saw this as a place of victory.

"This," he proclaimed, "is Horned Frog Hill. This will be our home. This will be where we build our team."

At first, none of us kids reacted. It was such a drastic change, most of us didn't know how to react. We had become so accustomed to the old way, it felt odd being shown such kindness and respect. Like an outside dog being invited indoors for the first time, we remained at the entryway. It sure looked nice on the other side, but we were still apprehensive. We weren't quite sure this wasn't some elaborate trick and at any moment the other shoe would drop, and things would go back to the way they were before.

After Coach Hall's initial speech, which probably hadn't gone over as well as he had hoped, we began a seemingly endless number of sprints, bear crawls, and buddy carries up the hill. That at least felt familiar. But it wasn't like before. Something was very different. We weren't being ridiculed and belittled as failures. Instead, he was using the exercise as a mechanism for building character, encouraging us to drive forward and to help our teammates. If we felt tired, Coach would cheer us on, telling us we could do it. When we felt like giving up, he motivated us to give more. Before long, emulating his behavior, the other kids started to offer words of encouragement. It didn't feel like a punishment at all; it was more about us strengthening both our bodies and our minds as we grew together as a team.

When we finished, he again brought us together. We were exhausted, but excited having done far more than any of us thought possible. In a serious tone he asked why we wanted to play football, how we thought that the team could improve, and what goals we should establish. He was not asking the parents; he was asking *us*, and not in the patronizing way that adults sometimes speak to a child. He spoke to us like men and seemed to value our answers. In fact, this became a major theme of Coach Hall's leadership.

"I'm not here to teach you about football," he would say, "I'm here to teach you to be men."

This same theme followed through with each practice. Every week would begin with a discussion of some topic of manhood.

"This week we will focus on …" work ethic, resiliency, teamwork or sacrifice, you name it. Yes, of course we worked on various football skills. But that never felt like the focus. Instead, like a stone used to sharpen an axe, or bring a platoon together, we were using football as a tool to become better humans. It wasn't about the game; it was about discipline and hard work. It was about pushing through adversity and trusting in our teammates. We learned responsibility and resilience, fortitude and inner strength. Winning wasn't only about the points on the scoreboard; it was about giving everything you had each and every play.

Being a champion was a mindset.

And at the end of each practice, we would run Horned Frog Hill. The whole time, Coach would reinforce the lesson of the day. Repeatedly, we would pore over each principle again and again as we forced ourselves to be faster, stronger, better. Unlike before, we were not running as a punishment. We were running because we were men, and real men strive for excellence. This distinction made all the difference. Victory was still important, but it wasn't winning for winning's sake. Rather, it was about giving a perfect effort and learning from our mistakes. It was about being the best we could be. Indeed, there were times when Coach would get upset, but this was always linked to some failure of discipline or effort and had nothing to do with the score. And it was equally as likely that a win would elicit this response if we did not perform at our potential.

Slowly, the culture of the team began to change. Football wasn't even the focus, but rather excellence in all things. If you improved at a skill, Coach would acknowledge you. If you respected your parents, you got to be a leader for the day. And even if you earned good grades, you were recognized in front of the team. By focusing on these extraneous activities, our level of commitment and performance increased beyond all measure. Because, at their core, it was about having the heart of a winner.

What does it mean to be a winner? We've all been on a variety of teams and organizations; it's easy to see at a glance which has a winning mindset. Obviously, there is some amount of skill that plays a major role, but there's also something more than that, an x-factor. Some people think that perhaps individuals are just born with excellence, endowed with tremendous luck that leads them to consistent victory. But at a young age I learned a powerful truth on Horned Frog Hill that should ring true to us all. Winning is not what makes a winner. Being a winner creates the result of winning. It is the character and drive, the consistent focus and will to improve that ultimately leads to being successful. Being a winner is a mindset that leads to lifelong success, both on the fields of friendly strife as well as on the battlefield of life.

The most important thing you do as a leader is to create a culture. Too many leaders get swept up in myopically focusing on efficiency and finishing tasks that they completely lose sight of who they are becoming. Yes, absolutely, mission accomplishment is tremendously important. But who you are when you accomplish the mission is equally, if not more, important. Besides, you have a built-in safety net of NCOs who are absolute experts at getting the job done. I promise you, if you pass off a challenging problem to some good NCOs, you can guarantee they're going to go way above and beyond in getting it solved. It's your job, however, to focus on what kind of culture you are manifesting.

Everything you do, or in many cases don't do, as a leader has an effect on the culture of your organization. There are literally entire books written on how to best create a positive culture. You could spend your whole life studying and still not learn all the ins and outs. Nevertheless, I've tried to simplify your efforts into three main steps for building a positive culture within your team: contemplate, communicate and cultivate.

Contemplate: if you want to impact the culture, you need to think about it. A positive culture doesn't accidently occur; it takes consistent, focused effort and attention. In a platoon, you have at least five dedicated NCOs thinking seriously about how to accomplish any given mission. But if you aren't actively considering what kind of culture you are creating within your team, assume that no one is. You must clearly establish a vision for what a "good" climate means. Everyone knows a good culture when they see it but few take the time to think deeply about what that actually means. Be specific. Even better, write it down with precise language. Then, set aside time regularly in your schedule to contemplate the state of your organizational climate and develop strategies for how to move towards the vision you've established.

Coach Barry and Coach Hall are excellent examples of this principle. In one case, you have a man solely focused on performance with flagrant disregard for culture. In the other instance, you have a man who had earnestly and consistent thought about the type of organization he was running.

Communicate: you must communicate your vision to the rest of your unit. Every single person must have a clear understanding of the values and expectations of the organization, a concept much easier said than done. A witty, well-written memo posted at the CQ desk isn't going to cut it. You need to engage and reinforce your message constantly. Seriously, it's going to feel like you're saying the same things over and over, but you will be shocked at how long it takes for that stuff to sink in. But over time, with regular bolstering, your message will begin to take root. Also, don't forget to seek buy-in from your troops. When your team feels a part of the decision process, it much more quickly goes from *your* vision to the team's vision of success. Moreover, by seeking your subordinates' feedback on establishing values, you are implicitly, if not covertly, compelling them to think deliberately about this challenging but valuable topic.

Ultimately, through regular two-way communication with your team, you can establish a clear set of values known to everyone in the organization. Through seeking input and consistently reinforcing the concepts valued on the team, Coach Hall was able to completely transform an unorganized, unfocused group of individuals into a cohesive, unified team focused on a shared vision. When asked "Who are we?" everyone would shout in response "Horned Frogs!" fully understanding what the name entailed.

Cultivate: having communicated and established a shared vision throughout the organization, you must ensure to cultivate a positive culture through regular, thought-out engagements. Think about a farmer trying to grow his crop. Preparing the land and planting the seed is absolutely a major part of the process, but the job is far from complete. The crop requires regular watering and feeding. Weeds need to be pulled and pests kept at bay. The farmer must protect and watch over their crop as it grows, nurturing it to a ripe maturity. So, too, must you grow the positive culture of your team. Find innovative ways to identify and reward positive behaviors which further your vision.

Similarly, when folks inevitably stray from the righteous path, interject and correct the behavior. In the (hopefully) rare occasion that you have a truly toxic individual who is actively steering the group in a negative direction, find ways to correct, isolate, or ultimately remove the person from the group. Be careful to identify which plants need more nurturing and support … and which are weeds. Conversely, find ways to identify influential members of the organization and empower them to make positive, lasting change. Once your subordinate leaders begin to take an active role in furthering your vision in the absence of your direct oversight, you know you are well on the right path.

With regular maintenance and consistently implementing the ideas of contemplate, communicate and cultivate, you will ensure a powerfully positive culture which ultimately leads to better mission accomplishment.

The year prior to Coach Hall's arrival, our team lost every single game, most by shut out. Frankly, it was embarrassing, and we were the laughingstock of the town. But by the time I finished middle school, only six short years after he took charge of the team, we had completely transformed. We were undefeated for over two years, clear winners of the local and regional leagues, and ultimately won the Junior Midwest Football Championship.

After this great transformation, several other teams and even the newspaper reached out to determine the secret to our success. Coach was even invited to talk on a major news network about the amazing performance of his team. *What special drills had we worked on? What was our workout plan? How had we determined our offensive strategy?* Of course, all these things played a vital role in our victories. However, the ultimate key to our success was the culture we built on Horned Frog Hill. Being a part of a truly great organization, especially at such a young age, had a lasting and powerful impact on my life. Before I ever stepped into any real leadership position, I already had an innate, empirical understanding of how to develop a culture and be on a winning team. Such lessons were invaluable for me in later years. No doubt your soldiers, looking back on their experience under your command will reflect on how you have shaped their understanding of leadership.

But I've found the thing that tends to stick with people the most is the lasting bond of love that forms between those who serve together. We've all seen *Band of Brothers* and *Saving Private Ryan*. Regardless of having served in the military, every single person on this earth longs for someone they can count on. You don't even need to like the person to form such a bond; just to know that they'll have your back if you ever need them. Such relationships often blossom in the midst of a crucible; powerful bonds forged in the flames of shared combat. It's for this reason such relationships are often correlated with the military. My own experience down range was no exception.

5 ···· DON'T CUT THAT BELT

"We must live together as brothers or perish together as fools." – Dr. Martin Luther King Jr.

SSG Vance was an asshole. Now don't get me wrong, he was extremely competent and one of the finest medics I've ever met. But he was still an asshole. Brash, loud, surly, irreverent, extremely stubborn, and to top it all off, he complained. Constantly. And not in the trivial self-centered banter shared by all soldiers as they huddle around a burn barrel. No. His complaining was that of a deeper, more purposeful melancholy. There was always some major inefficiency or some unforgiveable inequity in the battalion taskings or some great training shortfall which would inevitably lead to the entire company's fiery demise. Bright and early every morning he would greet me—or rather *accost* me—with his frowning, leather face to pester me about some new transgression.

"It's bullshit, Sirrrr!" he'd hiss, always dragging out the last syllable and shaking his head as if he were trying to get a bad taste out of his mouth. No amount of rationalizing would appease him. Worst of all, he was usually right. The "thing" probably *was* bullshit. But as a lieutenant, my bullshit deflection capability was rather limited and sometimes you just have to grin and bear it. The problem was that SSG Vance never grinned.

In the fall of 2012, we deployed to Afghanistan in support of Operation Enduring Freedom. At the time, I served as company XO and had the responsibility of leading a small team known as the ADVON party to establish our company footprint. This is to ensure that all operational needs are up and running prior to the arrival of the main body. To this end, we brought the motor sergeant, operations NCO, the supply NCO, and of course our medic—SSG Vance.

By this point, I had been with the unit for about four months prior to deploying and we had developed somewhat of a rhythm. I knew my staff's capabilities and they knew my expectations. They would spend the days coordinating and establishing our footprint while I would synchronize with our higher headquarters and periodically check in on our crew. They were a great team and, while not everybody liked each other, they worked together seamlessly. Each man knew their role and did it well. I have found that soldiers—particularly NCOs—do their best work when given purposeful guidance and left to their own devices. Truly great leaders understand how to manage a balance between getting "involved" and allowing their subordinates the freedom to excel. Too much oversight and soldiers get resentful of being micromanaged. Too little and people become complacent or worse. But finding a "baby bear" approach certainly requires a great amount of trust and is often challenging for younger officers to the chagrin of seasoned NCOs.

Summertime in Afghanistan was unreasonably hot. Devoid of any vegetation, the dry and rocky landscape offers no shade or reprieve from the unforgiving sun. Even the wind refuses to provide relief—like a drunkard belching in your face, the breeze was sickeningly warm and rank. Our uniforms were long-sleeved shirts, pants, and thick body armor. Over time, the sour smell of unwashed sweaty clothes combined with the noxious and inescapable odor of diesel fumes created quite a unique and pervasive olfactory experience. To this day, any time I get a whiff of truck exhaust, I'm instantly transported back to those days "downrange," where we lived in plywood buildings or prefabricated clamshell-tents.

Since it almost never rained, there was no functional need for any moisture protection-like siding and the government certainly wasn't going to waste money making the buildings aesthetically pleasing. So, almost all the structures were simple, flat, plywood boxes with no windows. Harsh and unforgiving with almost no signs of civilization, it felt ancient—almost prehistoric. The giant modernized Forward Operating Base (FOB) seemed odd and out of place against the outside world. You almost had the impression that we weren't only fighting the insurgents, but the land itself.

But despite the ugliness and cruelty of the days, I found beauty in the nights. In all my life, I have never witnessed a more spectacular night sky that could compare to what graced us each evening. The lack of civilization and modernity, which was a usual source of frustration, also enabled this star-filled marvel. With no lights, you could see billions of stars. Each night I would sit outside listening to the sounds of helicopters and gunfire and wonder at the awesome spectacle above. Like a sign from God, it posed a striking juxtaposition between the wickedness of the world below with the unfathomable beauty of the heavens above.

About a week into this set-up operation, one of the soldiers from our adjacent unit had been shot and we were instructed to observe how casualty care operations were conducted. SSG Vance and I grabbed our kit, hopped in our gator—a little 4-wheeler—and rushed to Charlie-Med.

We arrived a few minutes before the bird, so the head doctor invited us into a tent to get out of the sun while we waited. Someone pulled out a tin of dip, packed it, and held it out to the group. Everyone huddled around and reached in to grab a pinch, including the doc. The next few minutes we waited in mostly silence, only interrupted by nervous chit chat and the occasional *squirt* of someone spitting on the floor in the middle of the circle. Moments later, I could hear the *chop chop chop* of the helicopter fast approaching in the distance. All at once everyone burst into action, running around doing their last-minute checks. It was like a switch had flipped and all the joking and personality evaporated, morphing into mechanical laser focus. Finally, with a gust of wind, which I feared might knock down the tent, the bird landed. It was time.

The medical team rushed the injured soldier off the bird and into an old metal shipping container where they set him on a small table in the middle. There they quickly removed all his clothes and then carried him into the tent where we had been waiting. Once inside, they placed him on another table about ten feet in front of me. For a second, time seemed to stop. This pale naked boy of no more than twenty years of age laid stretched out before me with three gaping bullet holes in his leg. I turned to ask why they weren't taking him to the operating room. But then it hit me. We *were* in the operating room.

Have you ever seen a movie where someone gets shot and the doctor just reaches into the wound and plucks out the bullet with a pair of pliers? It was not like that—not at all. Apparently, it is necessary in these cases to create an incision along the fascia, a thin sack which surrounds muscles, to prevent harmful swelling. But in that moment, my tiny mind could not fathom any explanation to warrant the grotesque and bloody display before us. In this small canvas tent with dirt floors and no door, they utterly filleted this young man, peeling off his skin from ass to foot with amazing speed. I assumed the doctor had anesthetized the boy because he never moved, but it is possible he had passed out from the pain. Blood poured from the wound as medics raced to sop up the fluid from the young man's motionless body. With the boy's leg now splayed open like a perverse cannibalistic tableau, the doctor finally began his work to deftly remove the bullets.

One by one, he plucked the metal shards from the boy's leg with a little tug. You could hear the sharp *tink* of the doctor dropping the fragments into a metal basin. Then, having removed all obtrusions, the doctor sewed the boy's flesh back together with amazing speed. The whole while I stood there with my mouth agape, bile rising into the back of my throat. Later, the surgeon would explain this procedure was commonplace and necessary to prevent internal damage or something to that effect. But at the time I simply couldn't fathom what was going on or why the hell they would let us be there to watch.

They finished the surgery and transferred the young man to a different tent to recover and stabilize before he would be transferred to a larger care facility. As we were leaving, someone handed us a bag filled with his clothes to take back to his unit. Besides being covered in blood, I noticed that every single article of clothing had been cut in two. SSG Vance explained that this was the fastest way to get the soldier undressed and was common operating procedure for medics. It seemed to make sense for the most part, but it struck me as immensely odd that they would cut through his belt. The belts we wear are thick nylon and it seemed reasonably simple to just undo the darn thing, not to mention these little strips of fabric are outrageously expensive. The poor guy had just been shot and now he also had to buy a new belt.

"If I ever get hit, promise me that you won't cut my belt," I joked to SSG Vance, showing off my high-speed rigger strap around my waist.

"Negative, sir. That belt has got to go," he snorted back.

The following months passed by inexorably. The rest of the company arrived with no major issues. There were tragedies and triumphs, continuous missions, care packages, and field chow. Occasionally someone would buy a pirated copy of a new blockbuster from the local market. The guys from the company would all huddle around to watch a blurry version of a Hollywood hit. But for the most part, every day was the same, especially for the staff—work out, call up reports, track missions, and file upcoming CONOPS. Occasionally, I would sneak away from my duties to ride along on patrol with some of my PL buddies. They didn't really need me, but I'd spent my whole adult life preparing to go to war and I wasn't about to spend that time hiding away on the FOB. But those opportunities were few and far between.

The only exception to our otherwise dull existence were the almost daily mortar attacks. At first, the intense shriek of the early-warning alarm would send chills down my spine. We would dive to the floor or run for cover if it were close enough. Then, in tense silence, we would wait for the incoming munitions. In the distance, you could hear the soft thud of the rounds impacting sporadically around the FOB. Occasionally, a blast would be especially loud, and you could feel the ground shake beneath you. Everyone in the vicinity would look at each other anxiously, all thinking the same thing. Eventually, someone would quip something like "well that was close," and we would all chuckle nervously at the macabre joke.

But even the electric fear of the continual mortar attacks became almost commonplace after a few weeks. Sure, you still took cover, but the intensity of these moments seemed to fade. You could always tell who was new to theater by how freaked out they got in response to the alarm. Eventually though, everyone comes to grips with the fact that worrying does no good. You are either going to get hit or not, and there is nothing you can do to change it. You either accept it or you go nuts. So, despite the regular inconvenience of a mortar attack, the staff and I kept grinding away at the daily minutia.

Throughout this time, my relationship with SSG Vance seemed to evolve. He was still the same son-of-a-bitch he'd always been, but our shared experience of witnessing the gruesome surgery had brought us together. It was as though some great invisible weight was hidden above us, but together we helped to shoulder the other's burden. The fact that I had not buckled under the pressure was also a sign to SSG Vance. I had passed the test and was worth his regards. Now, don't misunderstand. We still argued, perhaps more than ever, now that we were in a deployed environment. He was still surly and offensive, but his overall demeanor seemed to soften ever so slightly. He started to smile and even laugh on rare occasions. He still showed up at my door first thing in the morning but instead of getting berated by an onslaught of complaints like before, I was pleased to find him with a fresh cup of joe each morning. It became our ritual to sit and sip our coffee as we discussed the upcoming events for the day. A mutual respect had grown between us.

Young as I was, he began to acknowledge that I was not without merit. Though he would never be so sentimental as to say the words out loud, he seemed to have made a mental pronouncement that I was a "good egg" and worth his time. Similarly, I began to see that SSG Vance was not a complete jerk. Gruff and opinionated as he was, he was also hard working, knowledgeable, and even had a bizarrely dark sense of humor once you got to know him. Most importantly, he was fiercely protective of those he deemed in his inner-circle and, thus, in his care.

As the weeks passed, I could tell that I was slowly gaining access into this sacred, inner sanctum of acceptance by SSG Vance. Though it may have been my imagination, I could swear he would brighten a bit when we would pass each other. The tension between us, which before had been genuine, morphed into a comedic ruse, as each of us teased the other with no real bite to our words. That day in the surgical tent, too potent for us to discuss in earnest, became a common morbid joke between us.

"How you doin'?" I would ask as we met each other at the start of each day. His response was always the same.

"Just thinking about cutting that belt, sir," he would jest with a sardonic smile.

Even on our worst days, when the necessities of combat seemed too much to bear this little joke helped to pull each other up and out of the darkness of our thoughts. I began to see SSG Vance as more of a mother-hen figure. The image made me laugh, but at its core, there was truth to the analogy. Always the protector, it wasn't enough for him to ensure soldiers were physically healthy, SSG Vance would make a point of checking out their mental wellness too.

One day, five or six months into the deployment, I received a long-awaited package from my wife containing a jar of gourmet peanut butter. With supplies limited, it is common for soldiers to develop cravings for certain foods or products that are unavailable in country. For some it is scented shampoo, for others it's their momma's fresh baked cookies. But for me, it was specialty peanut butter. Feverishly, I opened the box. It had been nearly two weeks since my wife had sent me a picture from the grocery store of the delectable sounding "limited edition honey-maple peanut spread." Since that moment, the idea of that sweet and salty confection loomed in the back of my mind constantly. At one point, I think I even started to dream about peanut butter.[3]

Unable to wait another second, I eagerly unscrewed the cap to the jar, hands shaking with anticipation. Then, regaining my composure, I decided to savor the moment. Slowly, almost sensually, I peeled back the thin plastic seal. A wave of rich, peanuty goodness flooded my nostrils. My mouth began to water in anticipation. Finally, overcome with desire, I plunged my spoon into the irresistible beauty of the unblemished treat, pulling out a huge, dripping dollop of pure confectionary bliss. As I raised the spoonful to my lips, I closed my eyes and prepared for certain ecstasy.

Wait. Something was off. I opened and closed my mouth a few times, confused. My mind felt fuzzy, and it was hard to think. Where was the peanut butter? I tried to reach out for it, but nothing happened. Was I lying

---

[3] I realize this is weird, but that's life downrange.

down? I tried to sit up, but again, I stayed motionless. Why couldn't I move? Why couldn't I see?

Franticly, I willed my eyes to open, and my vision slowly came back into focus. I could see a group of men in long white coats walking past me in a lengthy, clean hallway. I saw the shining white subway tiles along the wall sliding past me, breaking every few seconds as we passed another doorway. A feeling of vertigo washed over me briefly as I tried to make sense of my surroundings rushing by. Then, the nausea abated as I realized I was being pushed down the hall on a moving bed. Straps held down my legs, waist, and chest to keep me from being jostled around as we moved. Beyond the doorways were brief glimpses of very neat and identical little rooms.

Where the hell was I?

And where was my damn peanut butter?

I had been injured in a mortar attack while sitting at my desk. Though not hit by any shrapnel, the blast had knocked me unconscious and ruptured something in my spine. I had been rushed through Charlie Med— presumably to the same tent that they had performed surgery on the boy— and evacuated to a hospital in Germany. Of course, I didn't know any of this at the time and had to discover the details later by reading sworn statements and talking to some of my buddies. Apart from fleeting, dream-like memories (see *Jumpmaster*) I don't remember anything about the event. In fact, the whole peanut butter thing had taken place nearly two weeks before I was injured. Apparently, I ate the whole jar in one sitting. But to this day I don't have the vaguest clue what it tasted like.

My time at the hospital in Germany went by in a haze. With all the medication, I was constantly in and out of consciousness. Had I slept for an hour or several days? I couldn't tell. It also became hard to know what was actually happening. Dreams and reality blurred together. One moment I would be listening to the nurse going over my vitals and the next I would be back in Afghanistan running for cover. Then the scene would change and I would find myself standing over the body of the boy in the surgical tent. But this time, he was crying out in pain. With a gasp I would wake, covered in sweat to find myself back in the hospital bed. Then, after calming down I would fall back asleep and begin the cycle again.

Eventually, after an indeterminate amount of time I was considered stabilized and shipped back to the states. Once back in the good old U.S. of A., I was sent to Walter Reed Army Hospital. There I received spinal surgery to repair the damage that had been done (see *Pirate's Gold*). Thanks to the grace of God and the skill of the surgical team, it looked like I would make a full recovery. Following a grueling round of painful physical therapy, I was ultimately released from the hospital and returned to my home station.

As you might expect, there was a huge outpouring of support and well-wishes from my friends and family. Get well cards flooded our inbox and every night we were greeted by a new casserole prepared by someone in the Family Readiness Group (FRG). Then one day a series of thick plastic tuff boxes arrived at our front door. It was all my deployment gear which had been inventoried and shipped back, which is standard protocol. We brought them inside, but I did not open them. Coming home had been like waking from a strange dream; one moment I was in a war zone and the next I was in my living room. It was too surreal. With every fiber of my being, I had been trying to detach myself from the world and ignore the whole affair. But to look inside those boxes would be to admit the truth and acknowledge everything that had happened. I had been sent home early—without a purple heart, mind you—while my brothers were still fighting. There I was, enjoying the comforts of home, while they were still in harm's way. And to make it worse, part of me was glad.

I was glad to be rid of the heat and dust and constant stress of deployment. I was glad to be back to my wife and child and comfy bed. But I hated that part of me, the part that was fragile and selfish. If only I had been stronger. But I was too weak. Too weak to finish the mission and too weak to stay in the fight. I had failed. I was a failure. It was simply more than I could bear. And so, I escaped into the banality of everyday life, attempting to suppress the darkness of my thoughts by pretending like nothing had happened. But despite my mental efforts, the boxes loomed in the corner, serving as a constant reminder of the truth. Finally, after being lovingly prodded by my wife to remove the mountain of boxes cluttering our living room, I decided it was time. I waited until she was out of the house and hardened myself for the task. My hands began to shake, and tears started to well up in my eyes. I still have no idea why something so straightforward could be so difficult. But it was.

I took a deep breath and slowly undid the latch preparing to face the demons that had haunted me. Hesitantly, I lifted the thick plastic lid and peered inside. The house was quiet as everything in my periphery faded into nothingness. All that existed was the box. I quickly scanned through the heap of camouflage clothing. There, atop the pile, protruded a combination of metal and nylon. It was my belt, or at least a piece of it. Realizing I had inadvertently forgotten to breathe, I exhaled dramatically. A thin scrap of paper fluttered in the air and caught my eye. Cautiously, I inched closer to take a better look. Attached to the buckle of my belt was a small note from SSG Vance.

Despite the arguments, the complaining, and being a constant pain in my ass, SSG Vance had my back. At my lowest point, both physically and emotionally, this man who had been such a source of frustration took care of me like my life was on the line. Like *his* life was on the line. Apparently, he was the first to find me after the attack, sprinting to my office to check on me after he saw the smoke. Then, after making sure I was alive, he carried me to the vehicle before rushing to the medical tent. I'm a super big dude, easily over 300 pounds with all my kit on. Sometimes, I find myself imagining SSG Vance, small but fierce, leather faced and scowling with determination, as he rescued me. Why on earth would he do that?

The answer—he loved me. I wasn't his friend or his buddy, we didn't even like each other. But I was his brother and as such, he loved me. To like someone means that you enjoy being around them. But to love someone involves something deeper, a connection between souls. This beautiful and mystifying aspect of the human condition is a blessing that stretches throughout all of human history. The bible refers to this as *philia*, one of the Greek words for love. This philia is a love of respect, a love that is selfless and asks for nothing in return. It is unbreakable and compassionate. It causes you to stay up for hours, listening to and crying with your brother after they've lost a child. It causes you to drive across the country at the drop of a hat because your brother's house burned down, and he needs someone to sift through the ashes. And it causes a disgruntled medic to carry his giant LT, a guy he didn't really even like, nearly a mile to get him help.

Everyone needs to feel this bond of philia, to know we can count on someone when we are down. We need to be a part of a family. We need somewhere safe and permanent, a place that will accept and protect us no matter what is going on or what we have done. Such a space and relationship allows us to grow and flourish, and to push ourselves outside our boundaries and try something new. Something great.

As Theodore Roosevelt said in his famed "The Man in the Arena" speech, "There is no effort without error and shortcoming." And so, when we strive, we know we will stumble. For many, the fear of falling can be overwhelming and cripple them from ever straying from the safety of their mediocre path. But to have someone—to have a brother—who will pick you up when you fall and literally carry you to safety can give you the courage to move forward. Who is that person for you? Who is that battle buddy? Who is the person that, when it is midnight and the chips are down and you aren't sure you can go on, you could call and know they are going to answer? Perhaps a family member just popped into your head. That is awesome but set them aside for a moment. Who else is there?

Maybe you have that strong relationship and already know the comfort and confidence it can bring. They might not even be physically close, you might not have talked for months, but just knowing they are somewhere out there fills you with relief. Maybe you are truly blessed and have multiple relationships like this. Or, maybe, in this moment of reflection, your mind runs blank. As you scan through the thousands of online "friends," you may find yourself hard-pressed to picture someone who is really there for you, no matter what.

If you happen to find yourself in this last category and are struggling to think of someone with whom you can rely on in the way that I've described, do not despair. For those who want to build such a relationship, or perhaps you want to create more of these relationships, there is hope. But before you try to find someone to be there for you, first ask yourself—who can say you are there for them? Do people know that if they called upon you, you would answer? Relationships of this type are, in part, built upon mutual sacrifice. They aren't contractual—I'll do this for you, if you do that for me. These relationships are a covenant—no matter what you do, I will be there for you.

But it goes both ways. Such sacrificial relationships are implicit within organizations like the military. When you show that you are literally willing to put your life on the line to save someone, you've pretty much codified that relationship in stone. But, baring those rare circumstances, we need a more practical application for everyday life. You don't need to jump on a grenade to show people you care about them. All you must do is be there when they need you. When the group screws up something at work, you take the hit to protect your teammates. When your neighbor is swamped with their new baby, go cut their grass and ask for nothing in return. Give of yourself continually to those around you, even to people you don't necessarily like. Jesus didn't tell us to *like* our neighbor, he told us to *love* our neighbor. So be the person you wish you had in your life. Give until you feel like you have nothing left, and then give some more. I promise, you'll receive far more than you ever could have asked or imagined.

Back in my living room, I sat for several minutes staring at the small slip of paper. Trembling, I clutched the note, ripping it from the metal buckle sticking up from the jumble of clothes, and brought it close to my eyes to read. In bold, scribbled handwriting it read:

> *I've got you covered, sir.*
> *—SSG Vance*

Carefully, pensively, I reached out and began to extract the thick nylon strap as though I was pulling Excalibur from the stone. As it came into the light, I began to weep.

The belt was intact.

Understanding the interworking and mechanics of a good team is paramount to your success as a leader. First, you must look internally and clearly articulate your calling, both to yourself and those around you. With that established, you may assist others in cultivating their own sense of purpose. Provide a home, a place where like-minded individuals rally around these common values. Allow them to earn their place amongst an elite team, providing encouragement and training as they grow towards excellence.

Most importantly, be deliberate in how you manifest the culture of your organization. Such action, though seemingly intangible, will have the largest ramifications over the performance of the team as well as the lives of your teammates. Ultimately, when done well, building the team enables you and yours to enjoy the blessed comfort in the bonds of philia, knowing there is always someone there to watch your back.

···· **PART TWO: YOUR PAST BECOMES YOUR PRESENT**

6 ···· HOLLOW

*"We shall squeeze you empty, and then we shall fill you with
ourselves."* – George Orwell, *Nineteen Eighty-Four*

We are all damaged, every one of us. We are marred by scars and bruises
from distant battles, baggage we carry around from trauma. Perhaps such
challenges occurred long ago in our childhood, a painful memory looming
in the back of our minds. Or, perhaps, it occurred more recently. The harsh
sting still lingers brightly in our thoughts, like a red welt after a smack
across the face. In either case, such events most certainly change us,
temporarily driving us off the path we are meant to walk. To fully become
our best selves, we must identify these things from our past that are
holding us back. And only then, once we've named them, can we truly rise
above.

Sometimes these are big things—huge looming boulders thrust upon
our backs causing us to bear the weight of the world like Atlas. Other times

79

these wounds are smaller, like paper cuts, a lesser but constant irritation of a painful memory. No doubt there have been many such abrasions in your life, both big and small, which if left untreated can fester.

For me, one of these painful times started in fifth grade. That's when I became consciously mindful of how I looked. And even more important, that others were aware of how I looked. Until that point, I had always been this super skinny little boy with boundless energy pinging off the walls at every turn. Even when forced to sit still, usually through the compulsion of an irritated adult, I was never actually motionless. Instead, I sort of vibrated up and down like a bouncy ball just before it comes to rest, humming with a million frantic, short little jumps. That was me, pretty much all the time. Unless I was sleeping, I was moving.

Exercise and nutrition were farthest from my mind. I was too busy buzzing from one activity to another, like a hummingbird trying to inspect every flower before the end of the day. And, like the hummingbird, I also lacked the attention span to focus on any deep, existential concepts like how I am perceived by the world. So, it just never occurred to me that my appearance was something I should care about. So, I just kept buzzing along through life, blissfully unaware that those things mattered at all. All that buzzing around made me hungry. This, in fact, might be the only long-standing thought in my young adolescent, hummingbird mind—food. Always in the back of my mind, I was aware of an insatiable hunger and tried to quench this desire by sneaking snacks and treats whenever I could. So, perhaps there were three states of being for my childhood—sleeping, moving, and eating.

During our summers, I would stay with my grandparents. Grandpa had little patience for my high-energy lifestyle and had no problem letting me know it. Throughout our stay, I'd spend most of my time outdoors, enjoying the sunshine and surrounding wilderness of the farm, but also to stay away from Grandpa's stern sensibility.

Occasionally, Grandma—the embodiment of love and femininity—would sneak out to give me snuggles and fresh baked cookies before sending me back out into the surrounding fields to play. But eventually, the sun would hang low on the horizon, golden beams of light piercing through the tall grass in the fields, and I'd know it was time to head back to the house for supper.

And what a feast! Suppertime was a magical event in my eyes. Grandpa might have reigned over everywhere else on the farm, but the kitchen was Grandma's domain, and she made the rules with impunity. At her table, everyone got to eat as much as they wanted. It was heaven. After a full day in the kitchen, Grandma would emerge with huge mounds of fluffy mashed potatoes, thick slabs of juicy steak, flakey biscuits, and a homemade apple pie for dessert. I'd pile my plate high with delicious food and then, having loaded the vessel to capacity, cover everything in sumptuous gravy. No guilt, no shame, no restraint, and certainly not a vegetable in sight; just the pure bliss of homemade brown gravy covered love incarnate.

Grandpa would look on apprehensively, undecided on whether to be upset that I was eating up all their hard-earned food supplies or to be in awe of the impressive quantity I was able to digest.

"Lord Almighty, he's got a hollow leg!" Grandpa would exclaim after watching me eat every bit as much as him, if not more. "Where's he to put it all?"

"Now, now dear, he's a growing boy," Grandma calmly responded, with a loving pat on my back.

Grandpa, shaking his head, gave out a final exasperated declaration.

"I'm telling you, the boy's got a hollow leg," and he leaned over and gave me a little pinch on the thigh for good measure.

Grandma started to respond, but I jumped up on my chair and gave my thighs a swift smack.

"It's okay, Grandma," I shouted. "Grandpa's right, I can eat as much as I want 'cause I'm hollow!"

Blissful, carefree, and ignorant—that's how it was for years. Grandma was right though, sure enough I was a growing boy. I grew and grew and grew. I grew until I was eleven years old and kind of chunky.

"Baby weight," they called it. "Big boned," they said. But let's be honest, I was fat. Crazy as it might seem, but apparently you can't spend years eating mountains of butter-ladened food without paying the caloric consequences.

"This is a phase," they said. "It's always like this, out and then up. It's how kids grow. He'll probably have a growth spurt coming." That's what they said. And by "they" I mean my family; people who loved me unconditionally.

Other children, however, had a different perspective. The summer after fifth grade, I walked into the water park with high hopes, smiling from ear-to-ear despite my best attempts to play it cool. In one hand, I held a small neatly wrapped box containing a Beany Baby cow named "Mooosly." I remembered from years prior, back when Heather and I were closer, that she had a unique affinity for cows; they reminded her of her grandpa's farm. So, when I saw the plush, bean-stuffed toy at the store, I knew it was the right gift for her.

Gosh, I was so in love with her. Once, back in third grade, we had been close friends. Sadly, as time went on, things had become complicated and we'd grown apart. But now that we were more mature, and about to be sixth graders, this was my chance to reconnect.

With my free hand, I again reached into my pocket, fingering the invitation to the party. I recall my feeling of surprise and excitement after I found the small, red envelope on my desk after lunch. Until that point, I thought our paths had diverged forever, but perhaps this was a sign she was ready to give it another shot. As I passed through the main lobby and into the park, I surveyed the crowd. I didn't see anyone I knew. My heartbeat quickened and for a brief moment, I considered the possibility that I had come at the wrong time. I didn't want to be one of those lame kids whose parents drop them off at parties, so I had elected to walk to the park. The pool was just across the street from my house, but that was inconsequential. It could have been 100 miles away and I still would have walked. It was Heather-*freaking*-Jacobs after all, the most beautiful girl on the face of the planet.

Nevertheless, the idea that I had erroneously calculated the time needed to walk to the park was worrisome. For the millionth time, I pulled the now worn piece of paper out of my pocket to read the invitation again. It was supposed to start at noon. Slowly, making sure I correctly read each word, I re-inspected the note and looked at my watch. 12:11. Perfect, just like I had planned. Late enough that I didn't seem too eager, but not so late that I missed all the fun.

Still, where was everyone?

I walked a bit deeper into the park and out of the corner of my eye noticed a bundle of balloons blowing in the wind. On the table beneath the balloons was a stack of presents and a large, hand drawn poster that read, "Happy Birthday Heather." That must be it! As I walked closer, I recognized Heather's mom sitting at the table and rushed over to say hello.

"Oh, it's so nice to see you again," Mrs. Jacobs said, reaching out to give me a hug. Years before, back when we had been better friends, I was a regular at Heather's house. But that was some time ago.

"The other kids already went off to ride the new waterslide, but they'll be back for cake as soon as they're done."

I followed her pointing finger to see the giant staircase to the new slide reaching up into the heavens. Leading out from the staircase stretched a humongous line. The entire town must have come out to try the new slide.

"Thanks, Mrs. J," I said, carefully placing my small, wrapped, token of affection down on the table with all the other presents.

Quickly, I stripped down to my trunks, dropping my shirt and sandals into one of the cubbies, and started briskly walking towards the giant line. Stupid, stupid! I thought. I was so concerned with trying to play it cool, that I had totally missed my opportunity to be with the group. Surveying the line, I saw the gaggle of kids midway up the slide on a balcony, just past a long skinny staircase. There was no way I was going to be able to get to them, or was there? I saw that the balcony connected to the concession stand, which in turn connected to the upper terrace of the park. If I could get up there, I might be able to hop through and slip in line with the rest of the group.

Walking as fast as possible without bringing on the wrath of the lifeguards, I hustled to the upper terrace towards the concession stand. It looked like they had built a new, back entrance into the wall so that patrons, hungry from waiting in line for the slide, could sneak in and grab a bite or use the restroom without losing their place. As long as I could get there before the group had moved too far past, I should be able to slip in unnoticed and without a problem. Thoughts of Heather swam through my mind. I imagined her jumping into my arms with joy as I miraculously appeared from the hidden doorway—her birthday saved. Well okay, maybe not that, but I hoped she would at least be happy to see me.

I burst through the doorway and onto the small balcony adjacent to the staircase, a bit faster than I should have but I was too excited. I took a moment to catch my breath and regain my composure, surveying the crowd hoping to find Heather's enchanting smile. There! Her head was turned away, but I'd spent countless hours pining for Heather during class and could even recognize her from the back of her head. I took a step closer and was about to say "hi" when I heard a noise.

"Oh my gosh, he actually came!" cried a shrill, nasally, familiar voice from off to my left. Elizabeth Wardel, Heather's nextdoor neighbor and de facto best friend, stood at my periphery, mouth agape in faux surprise. In response to her exclamation, the group turned, following her pointed finger, to look at me. Elizabeth wasn't my favorite person, but at that point, I didn't really know her that well and figured it was best to be nice.

"Hi, Liz," I replied, turning to give her a small wave and a head nod. "Where's Heather? I want to say 'happy birthday.'"

Somehow, in the commotion I had lost her. I looked around again, hoping to see her familiar smile but instead saw a sea of sneering callous faces I did not really recognize. Besides Elizabeth, they were all middle school boys, a year older than us. I vaguely remembered seeing a few of them in the hallway in years past, but I don't think I had ever spoken to any of these kids, and they certainly weren't my friends.

"He actually came! Ha, ha, ha!" Elizabeth spat out again, not laughing but saying the word "ha" as she spoke.

I stared back, dumbfounded, not understanding what was happening.

"Of course, I came. Heather invited me," I offered, trying to clear up the apparent confusion. With that, the whole group burst into laughter, sharing a joke I didn't understand.

"You think our Heather would invite someone like you? Ha, fat chance," Elizabeth quipped, again with her mocking laugh. Drawing closer, like she was about to tell me a secret, but still talking loud enough for everyone to hear, she continued.

"No, I am the one who gave you the invitation." At that, she leaned back on her heels, crossed her arms and flipped her hair back, as though she had just revealed a devious plot. I still didn't understand.

"But … why?" I asked, now searching her eyes and those of the boys behind her for some semblance of compassion. Instead, they looked like sharks in the water, circling their prey after they smelled blood—something in their eyes seemed dangerous.

Where was Heather? Where was that smile and those kind eyes that had been my source of joy for so long?

"Because," Elizabeth snapped, "I wanted to see if they would let someone as fat as you into the pool without a bra." At that, the entire group erupted into laughter, one boy was actually rolling around on the floor of the patio.

"So where is it? Where's your bra?" she continued. "Ha, ha, ha."

Her staccato laugh boomed in my head like someone driving nails into my coffin. I could feel my pulse quicken and my face grow hot. *What was happening? Heather didn't invite me? And something about a bra?*

"Dude, check out his big boobs," cried out one of the shark-eyed boys. "They're so bouncy."

"He even came from the concession stand," another boy joined in. "Hope he left some food for us!"

I looked down at my body, as though I were seeing it for the first time. *Was I fat?* It was honestly something I had never even considered. *No, I was just big boned.* That's what Grandma said—just big boned and a growing boy. I looked at the other boys and then back at my own flesh.

"Bouncy," they had said.

"Fat," they had said.

Involuntarily, I brought my hands up to my stomach and chest, and squeezed, feeling the flesh give way and squish in my fists. I looked back at the other boys, boney and hard. They weren't squishy, only I was. Like Adam in the garden, I suddenly became tremendously aware of my nakedness. Shame and embarrassment washed over me, and I felt utterly trapped in my own body. I leaned closer to Elizabeth and in a small feeble voice again pleaded.

"Why?"

But she didn't answer. The thin smirk on her face grew into a wide, sinister smile as she stepped back into the crowd of boys.

"So," she said flatly. "I'll ask again. Where's your bra?" Then she asked again. And again. Each time placing emphasis on a different word.

One of the boys joined in, then another. Before long, the whole group was chanting in unison. I could feel tears welling up in my eyes and I knew if I didn't do something fast, I was going to start crying which would make things even worse. For a moment, I thought about charging into the group and punching the kids. I couldn't beat all of them, but I was pretty sure I could get one good hit in and maybe win back some of my pride. But as I scanned their twisted, maniacal faces looking for an easy target, I saw her. Through everyone, at the back of the crowd, was Heather. She was not chanting or laughing like the others. She just stood there quietly, looking down, an intense expression of both sadness and shame on her face. Sadness for having witnessed the broken heart of someone she once called a friend. And shame for her role in the subterfuge that put me in that position. That was the final blow—sadness and shame.

My insides were torn apart, ripped from my body, and I was left with a deep, cosmic emptiness. The entire experience had created a tiny black hole in my soul, the singularity sucking up everything inside me. I had no words to speak, no strength to fight. I had no tears to cry. Nothing but cold, hollow emptiness. So, without a word, I turned and walked away, only faintly noticing the jeering chants from the kids behind me. Grabbing my belongings from the small cubby, I threw on my shirt and hurried away from the park. I noticed that, for the first time, my shirt wasn't just clothing but a shield to guard me from the prying eyes of the outside world. I gave it a small tug, wishing it was bigger and hoping to stretch it out. Nevertheless, the fabric still felt too tight against my skin, a sensation I had never realized before. I pushed the thought out of my mind and tried to focus, replaying the events from the pool party as I walked home. I tried to be like a scientist, analyzing everything, trying to understand what exactly had happened and why. *What was the point of it all? And why were they so mean?*

Still, to this day, I find myself questioning the motivations for an event that remains one of the purest examples of unprovoked aggression. But in my heart, I know, just as I knew back then, why those kids would do such a thing. Evil exists. The devil is real. We, humans, are broken, vapid, hollow creatures who too often turn away from God's light and wander into the darkness. How many of those other children, the shark-eyed boys, were hurting? How many felt lost or ashamed or ridiculed for their own shortcomings? What was behind Elizabeth's mask of ice and venom?

Her father had abandoned her and her family two years prior; she was empty, broken and hollow. And so, she lashed out, finding someone to transfer her pain. Someone weaker and naïve; an easy prey to consume. For a moment, they all felt better, or at least they pretended to. Shrouding themselves in false superiority, they believed the lie that they were whole and happy. But truth is eternal and even the best self-deceptions fade with time. No amount of posturing would ever fill the void and hollowness within. Thus, they were stuck in a seemingly endless cycle of abuse and pain, lies and reality.

When I got home, I rushed straight to my room, not stopping to talk to my parents for fear of breaking down. Tears were for little boys. The child that had left for the party that day—the innocent, carefree boy I had been just an hour prior—might have had room for tears and nestled into his mother's embrace and cried himself to sleep. But that boy was gone. He never made it back home. I was changed. I was harder and more aware of the harshness of the world.

Once inside my room, I rushed to my desk and pulled out a scrap of paper and a pencil. In bold, harsh letters I scratched the name "Elizabeth Wardel" and taped it to my mirror. Then, I stripped off my shirt and stared at my reflection, then back at the name. I hated her and I hated myself. But I hated her more for making me hate myself. With clenched teeth, I shook my head in disgust and dropped to the ground.

In a rage-fueled trance, I started doing pushups. More and more, I kept pushing until my arms were sore and I collapsed to the ground from the effort. Despite my best attempts to hide them away, tears started to flow. For a moment, I laid flat on the floor, crying and in pain. I knew I couldn't fix my physique in a single day, but something about the effort and the pain made me feel better. It was like I could replace the deep emotional aching, something senseless and out of my control, with this physical pain, an agony of my choosing.

Wiping my face, I started doing more pushups, each repetition offered up like a sacrifice and cast into the bottomless, aching hole now at my core. When I truly couldn't do one more, I rolled over and began doing sit-ups in the same fashion. And when I again reached exhaustion, I cycled back to push-ups. On and on it went, back and forth, until my entire body shook with fatigue. But still I pressed on, determined to fill the hollowness inside me, determined to make myself hard and impervious and whole, determined to never be vulnerable enough to feel that way I did at the pool ever again. The trauma of that day left a wound that took years, possibly decades, to heal fully. And even after the sting of that moment had faded away and I was finally able to let go and forgive, the scar remained. For a long, long time I kept Elizabeth's name posted on my bedroom mirror.

After I finally hit that growth spurt Grandma always talked about and shed the "baby weight," Elizabeth was there. While in high school, after I was named 1st Team All-State for football, she was there. Even after I was accepted to one of the most prestigious and physically demanding universities in the world, she was *still* there. She was always there, *always* in the background, *always* watching and waiting; a constant reminder that if I stumbled, if I was ever slightly less than exceptional, she and others like her would be there to ridicule me.

But to be honest, I no longer hate her. I never really hated her. After all, she was just a sad, hurting little girl, lashing out at the cruel world that robbed her of a loving family. The person I despised was that fat, pathetic, naïve little boy who stupidly went to the party in the first place. How could he be so obtuse? How could he be so weak? And most of all, how could he let himself become that jiggly piece of human trash? That was not me, not the real me at least. He and I might share the same name, we might share the same body, but that wasn't who I was. And I didn't care how long it took, I was going to prove to everyone, most of all myself, that beyond a shadow of a doubt, we were not the same person. I wanted to erase him from existence. Every exercise, every sprint or repetition, each was a stab at his memory, attempting to kill the small, feeble child who hid within. But it went even deeper than that. It wasn't just the fact he had become so fat; it was that he was soft. He was vulnerable. It was so obvious what was happening, there were so many signs. How could he not have guessed? How could he not anticipate the attack? Like an idiot, he'd opened his heart completely only to have it crushed amidst the sound of laughter. But never again.

Each of us, in our own way, is a survivor of trauma. That doesn't make you a victim, necessarily, but it's a hard world out there and you are guaranteed some bumps and bruises. It takes on various shapes and forms, and some of us escape with less scar tissue. For the most part, I've been extremely fortunate in my life compared to others. But that doesn't mean such experiences don't affect us and change us. The world is broken. *We* are broken. Many of us try to sweep away the shattered pieces, pretending like nothing happened. Others wallow in the wreckage, unable to move past the injustice. Either way, the result is the same—we suffer. Such is the tragedy of existence, no one escapes unscathed. As we walk through life it's as though we were gathering painful rocks, each trauma is a jagged and heavy stone. Some are big, others are small, but each are weighing us down. All that is needed to lighten the load is to simply let go. Yet, we continue to hold tight onto our burden, too afraid that if we loosen our grip, we might lose ourselves.

What are you carrying around with you? What pain are you embracing, shrouding yourself in the agony of a memory hidden deep within? Sometimes these things can motivate us. You can use that anger as fuel, driving you towards greatness. I would never wish the heartache I experienced on anyone, but would I have achieved everything I did without it? Would I have pushed myself unceasingly? Would I have an insatiable need to be stronger? To be tougher? Maybe, maybe not. But I do know, had I let go long before, at least I would have been making my own path and I know I would have been much happier.

7 ···· LORD OF THE DUMBBELL FLIES

"Look well into thyself; there is a source of strength which will always spring up if thou wilt always look." – Marcus Aurelius, Meditations

Middle school gym class was a challenging time. I always considered myself athletic, strong and reasonably coordinated, but none of the gym class activities seemed to align with my skillsets. I was a blunt instrument, good at hitting, pushing, and throwing. I could move a tackling sled up and down the field by myself with little effort, but in an open field or in a footrace, I was slow as molasses. Unfortunately, all the gym class games were running-based and there wasn't a tackling dummy in sight. Each class we would go out to the soccer field or track, and despite my best efforts, I would get shown up by the smaller, faster kids. Once mercilessly teased for my above average size, I felt out of place amongst my slim and quick peers, running circles around me. I was several inches taller than all the other kids and at least 50 pounds heavier. Nevertheless, I felt like a small fish in the middle school P.E. pond.

Everyday felt like a nightmare as I slowly changed into my gym clothes, mentally and emotionally preparing myself for another day of feeling embarrassed. Then, on one fateful rainy day in middle school, our P.E. teacher decided to try something new. Hearing the rain crash down against the locker room windows, we were not surprised to learn outdoor activities were canceled. Several of the boys started lacing up their court shoes and getting hyped for the inevitable basketball games, which were our usual rainy day activity. A handful of the seasoned ball players started to banter over who was going to guard who and how many points each would score on all the non-basketball playing peons around them. And I was one of those peons, unable to hit or push any of the other players, I found myself tremendously unqualified to play the game. It didn't matter how hard I threw the ball; my total lack of finesse always left me underhanded and outmatched. Thus, for what seemed like the millionth time, I prepared myself for yet another physical and emotional blow.

Our gym teacher, whom everyone called "Coach," blew his whistle, the standard signal for us to group around him for initial instruction at the beginning of class. We all started moving towards Coach, pushing and shoving like normal as we clumped together in the crowded locker room. Some of the boys had already grabbed a few of the basketballs from the equipment closet, wanting to demonstrate to everyone how seriously they took the game. Over the buzz of conversation, you could hear a loud *thump thump* as they bounced the balls on the dusty concrete floor. Then, having allowed for the appropriate amount of rowdiness, Coach blew his whistle again. The crowd fell silent except for the occasional *thump* of one of the self-proclaimed "hoopers" periodically slamming a ball to the ground.

"All right, men," he began, walking us out of the locker room and onto the court. Here, the basketball bounces seemed to grow even louder, echoing off the walls of the large, mostly empty room.

"Today we're going to try something new," Coach continued once everyone had caught up. Everyone looked around with anticipation.

"You mean like one-on-one or something?" One of the basketball kids spoke up.

"No, no," Coach shook his head. "Not like that. In fact, put the dang basketballs away. Who told you to pull those out anyway?"

My head popped up. *No basketball?* I was intrigued. Despite being a head taller than the others, I involuntarily stood on my tiptoes and leaned in to hear Coach better.

"No, today I figured I'd show you our beautiful weight room!" he exclaimed, making a grand, sweeping gesture with his arm towards a door at the far end of the court. It was a door I had never noticed before.

Scanning my memory, I couldn't recall having ever seen it open. I guess I had always assumed it led to a closet or maintenance area or something. But today it was open and seemed to lead to a large, unexplored area of the school. Overcome with curiosity, we rushed into the weight room. Unlike the splendor of the pristine, shiny basketball court, the gym seemed totally dilapidated. The weights were rusted and mismatched. The benches were tattered and torn. Some of the equipment didn't even work while others were held together with duct tape. Still, something about the old, musty room called out to me. While the other boys sneered and giggled at the foreign and antiquated pieces of equipment, I beamed with excitement at the prospect of having found a place I might belong.

Coach began to walk us through the gym, pointing out each of the pieces of equipment, identifying its name, and what kind of exercises it could be used for. At each station, he would do a few repetitions and try to explain the correct technique required to maximize the benefit of the exercise while minimizing injury. But all of this was immensely boring to all the kids in the class. Well, everyone except for me. I felt like I was an explorer, discovering a brave, new world. The strange and exotic pieces of machinery filled me with excitement and wonder. Not everyone, however, shared my enthusiasm. People started yawning or staring off into the distance, others dropped all pretenses of paying attention and openly started having side conversations. Coach, seeing that he was losing the class, decided to change tactics.

"Ah, tired of all this boring educational stuff, I see?" he asked. "Ok, well who's up for a challenge? How's about we find out who's the strongest kid in class?"

All the heads in the class immediately snapped back towards Coach. If they hadn't been paying attention before, they were now. My middle school experience often felt like an excerpt from *Lord of the Flies*, and for many of the kids, the prospect of lording one's physical prowess over that of the other boys was intoxicating. Without hesitation, several of the other children ran up to take their turn at the challenge.

"Slow down, slow down," Coach cautioned. "Let me at least explain the rules first."

He went on to describe how we would be using the bench press as our exercise. By itself, the bar weighs 45 pounds. Each person was going to lay down on the bench and, in a controlled manner, bring the bar to his chest. After a brief pause, they would then press the bar back up to the starting position and Coach would help re-rack the weight. Throughout this process, Coach was behind us, acting as a spotter to ensure we didn't accidently drop the bar on our heads. If we were unable to complete the repetition on our own, he would assist us to get the bar up, but we weren't allowed to continue in the competition. Then, the next person would attempt the lift. Once everyone had given it their best shot, we would add more weight to the bar and everyone still in the competition was given another chance to try to lift the new, heavier weight. This cycle would continue until only one of us remained. He would be crowned champion.

Champion.

The word rang out in my head over and over. Man, I wanted it, I *needed* it! I needed to feel good at something, anything.

Please Lord, I silently prayed. *Please let me do well.*

One by one we filed up to the bench to attempt the lift, starting first with just the bar. Since we were going alphabetically, I stood in the middle of the line watching others take their turn. The long, thin piece of metal looked comical without the large plates on the ends as depicted in magazine images. It looked like a big toothpick. Surely, it would not be any real challenge. Still, to my surprise, some of my friends struggled to hoist the load. Seeing their distress, my heart quickened in anticipation, afraid to look weak in front of the other boys.

"Fat *and* weak," they would say.

I wasn't going to let them say that to me. *You can do this. You can do this!* I tried to mentally encourage myself. But despite my inner-mantra, I could feel the slimy hands of doubt creeping around the edges of my consciousness. Finally, it was my turn. I laid flat on my back and looked up at the ancient, stained ceiling panels, grabbing the bar as I had been shown.

"Ready?" Coach asked, holding the load at the starting position above my head. I gave him an apprehensive nod to indicate I was ready, and he slowly let go of the bar, letting me feel the entirety of its weight. A wave of surprise and relief washed over me.

This is easy, I thought, effortlessly completing the repetition. Making my way to the back of the line, I said a quick prayer of thanks; trying to remain humble allowed a brief spark of hope at the prospect of doing well in the competition. Around and around we went, the size of the line dwindled as more weight was added to the bar. Eventually, to my amazement, I found myself one of the remaining three competitors. The other two boys, Chris and Drew, were widely considered the most athletic amongst our peer group. Fast, determined, and hyper-competitive, both boys excelled in almost all gym class related events. On the field, Chris was a force to be reckoned with. However, off the field, he was reasonably nice to everyone, or at least he didn't go out of his way to be mean. Drew, on the other hand, was a total ass who used his abilities to browbeat others into submission. It wasn't enough to be better than you on the soccer field; he went out of his way to remind you he was simply a better person. You were inferior to him. Or at least that's how it felt.

I watched both these young men, faces contorted in anguish, as they struggled under the weight of the bench press. These titans of my youth, boys who represented the pinnacle of fitness and thus a source of tremendous pain and embarrassment at my inadequacy, were crumbling beneath the weight of the lift. A weight that I found to be quite easy. It felt so odd and out of place with the laws of the adolescent social hierarchy that I had come to know and, until that point, been imprisoned by. An idea came to me like a bolt of lightning.

This must be what it feels like, I thought. *This must be what it is like for them on the field. Watching everyone else struggle, watching me struggle, gasping for breath, while they effortlessly dart around.*

Something deep within me changed. What was previously dormant was now stirring and hungry. Like puzzle pieces snapping into place all at once, I suddenly realized, this is *my* thing. This is what *I'm* good at.

"More," I said.

The whole class looked on and cheered … 115 pounds … 135 pounds … 155 pounds … I kept pushing for more. Both Chris and Drew had dropped out long before. Drew angrily stomped off as though the whole thing was stupid and unfair. I kept shouting for more weight. I didn't want to just win, I wanted to leave no doubt that I was victorious. *I was the champion.* All those times that I felt slow and inferior and fat meant nothing now because here in this room I was king.

"More!" I shouted viscerally with a weird mixture of pain and anger and determination that I had never felt before filling my voice. As I got into position for my next lift, 205 pounds, the entire class erupted into hysterics. Shouts of encouragement burst from the small, sweaty room like primal, frenzied beasts. Even Coach joined in the uproar, shouting.

"Come on, son. Light weight! You got this!!" he yelled. The cries filled me with fire and, letting out my own lion-like roar, I pressed the massive load upward slowly, arms shaking with the effort. In the moments before I reached the top, as the bar inched further upward, the crowd grew completely silent, everyone holding their breath with anticipation. Then, as the bar racked back into place, an explosion of cheers burst from the small room.

It was pure anarchy.

Kids were screaming and running around. A few came over to slap me on the back or give me a high-five. Others stood there with their mouth agape, pointing at the weight, then to me, then back at the weight. Even Coach, who might have been the most excited of anyone, got in on the fun, yelling, "He did it! He did it!" as he grabbed my shoulders and shook me back and forth. It was all amazing and a bit unnerving. The sharp contrast between the intense, guttural rage, which I felt during the lift, now combined with this new outpouring of jubilation had me off balance and feeling an odd mixture of anger and accomplishment. For a few moments I stood there unsure, observing everyone else celebrating while internally trying to figure out what had just happened.

Then, the bell rang. It was time to go. Like Pavlov's dog everyone responded, subconsciously reacting to the sound, and started moving towards the door. The extreme excitement had died down, but as we made our way back to the locker room people continued to come up and congratulate me.

"Dude, that was epic!" Chris ran up beside me to clap me on the back. Drew was with him but stayed silent. Perhaps, conceding defeat to someone was a bit much for him. Still, he managed to throw up a small head nod and a half smile to indicate his mild agreement.

"Remind us to call you if we need something heavy moved," Chris continued. With another swat on the back, he and Drew ran ahead, not wanting to be late for their next class.

I just kept walking, though. The thought of classes couldn't have been further from my mind. I was still so caught up in everything that had happened, everything I had gained, that I didn't care about being late. In an instant I had rocketed into a new social stratum through the admiration of my peers, and most of all I had proven to myself that I *was* good enough. I had done it. I had *won*.

I was a winner.

I was the undisputed champion and it felt good. Not only had I beat Chris and Drew, but I obliterated them. And in the process, I seemed to have earned their respect. Not only had I broken the 200-pound barrier, which was almost unheard of for my age group, but I did not fail in any of my lifts. True, that last repetition was near the upper bound of my abilities, but as far as the other kids were aware, my strength was limitless. And, as far as I was concerned, they were right—my strength *was* limitless.

Everything felt different. *I* felt different. Any obstacles I had perceived seemed to melt away into nothingness and the world opened itself up to me. When I walked down the hall smiling, I noticed people laughing and smiling back. Friends stopped to wave and say *hi* as they scooped up their books from their lockers. I didn't feel nervous or guarded because it now felt like I was surrounded by friends. *Was this new? Was everyone being nice to me because of what happened in the weight room? Or had it always been like this, and I hadn't let myself notice?* Whatever it was, I liked it.

Still, something about the transformation puzzled me, but I couldn't quite put my finger on it. What about me had changed? It took years for the full weight of the idea to finally sink in, but eventually the answer became clear—nothing. Physically, at least, nothing had changed. I was exactly the same person before that day in gym as I was the day after. I was every bit as strong and capable. The only adjustment was how others treated me. It was only when they saw my capability that they treated me differently. And then, having received their praise, I started to see myself in a new light.

At that time in my life, I realized, I was incapable of truly seeing myself. I could only see the "me" that was reflected by others. They were my mirror, except distorted and perverse, shifting my image at their whim. When they said I was unworthy, I felt unworthy. When they cheered at my victories, I felt victorious.

But why do they get to be the sole deciders?

The world does get a vote. As much as we'd love to stay in the loving arms of our mommies, hearing how wonderful we are at everything, that is not how the world works—nor should it. Maybe there is something we aren't good at. Maybe there are lots of things. Regardless of our beliefs, the truth will manifest itself in the image reflected back at us by nature and by society. Sometimes that image is harsh, a painful reality we would rather not see. If you do not study, you receive a poor grade on the exam. If you skip leg-day, then the guys at the gym will point out your tiny baby chicken-legs. And when we fail to live honorably, then we stain our reputation and maybe worse. In the end, we all get our comeuppance. Like Dorian Gray's infamous portrait, this mirror can reflect back the grotesque self we try to hide away.

Nevertheless, sometimes that mirror is broken. Sometimes, we find ourselves looking into an image distorted not by our imperfections, but that of the world around us. We fail to see our true self, as we were meant to be, splendid and majestic, because our reflection is distorted by the shambled remains of a fallen world. Perhaps the obsessions of your micromanaging boss are a reflection of his own insecurities. The incessant digging by your peers might be an indicator of their own fears about their deficiencies, hoping to bring everyone down to their level. Maybe the bully of your youth was only replaying the abuse he faced at home.

Yes, whether we like it or not, reality gets a vote and we should listen to what it says. But it isn't the *only* vote. We must be resilient enough to take a hard, earnest look in the mirror and decide what is real. The blemishes we see … are they a true reflection of our own poor choices, or a false reality contrived by a damaged world? It is up to you to decide.

We are not perfect. We have flaws and are broken. If we take an honest look in the mirror, we *should* find plenty of blemishes and defects. But that is not the entirety of our identities. We have been designed by the Creator for something special, but our weakness and humanity can get in the way of achieving our purpose. Light and dark, good and bad—each of us is a combination. If we find that we are only seeing one side or the other, we're probably not being entirely truthful. No matter how much we wish the goal line was closer, or the score was higher, or that we were the fastest, strongest, best person that ever lived—it just isn't true. None of us gets to make up our own reality because it makes us feel better.

Sometimes, the truth can hurt. But truth is also real and virtuous and brings a promise of hope.

8 ⋯ PIRATE'S GOLD

"Not all treasure is silver and gold, mate." – Jack Sparrow, *Pirates of the Caribbean*

Beep, beep, beep. The rhythmic staccato chirps of the heart monitor trilled quietly in the background, steadily alerting the staff that, yes, I was indeed still alive. What had first been a source of annoyance, sharply jabbing at my eardrums, now seemed like a soothing drumbeat, fading out of my awareness amidst the cacophony of other random noises.

After I was injured in Afghanistan and before I returned home, I spent some time in Walter Reed National Military Medical Center. As I laid in the hospital bed, I focused and tried to identify each sound—a wet cough from a sick patient next door, nurses briskly rifled through papers and talked to each other in hushed tones, the metallic squeak of an old cart as a staffer went room to room delivering meals, two sets of footsteps as an elderly vet and his wife shuffled slowly down the hallway arm in arm.

How long had I been here? A few days? Longer?

It felt like I was in a fog, unable to concentrate as I dipped in and out of consciousness, jumping between reality and dreams. I listened for the beeps, anchoring me to the world, reminding me that I was awake and alive. In my periphery, I saw someone stirring. Turning my head I could see my wife, shifting in her chair, trying to find a comfortable position as she slept. It was dark outside; they must have let her stay through the night. On the table next to her I could see the white and blue folder, with the medical center's name embossed on the front. She was probably going over the documents again before falling asleep. They'd given us a huge packet of information detailing the specifics of my upcoming surgery, risk factors, follow-on treatment plans, and an endless list of further medical appointments. By now she'd probably memorized the damn thing, but my darling wife, always the planner, continued combing through the packet to make sure she identified and understood every detail.

Holy smokes, I didn't deserve her.

She's always good in a crisis, that's probably why she's such a good military officer. A hell of a lot better than me. Since getting notified of my injury after the mortar attack in Afghanistan, she'd gone into full combat mode, shedding her emotions and slipping into the role of steely-eyed military planner.

"There'll be time to freak out later," she'd said. "But right now, I have work to do."

Before I'd even gotten back to the states, she'd already arranged for childcare, scheduled my medical appointments, and was investigating physical therapy options for after my surgery. She's strong, that's one of the reasons I married her, but she shouldn't have to be this strong. It's supposed to be my job to take care of her, not the other way around. She shifted again in her chair, this time giving a little shiver against the cold night air.

In that moment I would have given anything to stand up and wrap her in a blanket, to kiss her forehead and tell her everything would be alright.

Just to move to her side and hold her hand to let her know she was not alone. But I couldn't. I couldn't move. I couldn't get out of bed. It wasn't supposed to be this way. *I was supposed to take care of her*.

The next morning one of the nurses went over the operation details.

"Alright, sir, do you have any questions? Spinal surgery is a big deal, but don't worry, I'm sure we'll get you put back together in no time."

An image of Humpty Dumpty flashed through my mind with all the king's horses and all the king's men dressed up in these blue-green scrubs. Also, why the heck would horses be doing surgery? That's weird right? And, have you noticed, nowhere does it ever say that Humpty is an egg, just some poor schmuck who fell off a wall? Brutal.

"So, any questions?" the nurse asked again, snapping me back into focus.

I shook my head. The way I saw it, I was just along for the ride at this point. My wife, on the other hand, interjected with pen and paper in hand and began reading the list of pointed questions she'd prepared. I laid my head back, stared at the ceiling, and went back to daydreaming. Apparently not wanting to disturb me, the two headed into the hallway.

I listened as their rapid footsteps faded down the long corridor of the military hospital. But then, in the distance, I heard a strange, unfamiliar sound. Step, *thud*. It wasn't like normal walking; the cadence was all off like they were off balance. Step, *thud*. Did they have a cane? The second step was loud and wooden. Step, *thud*, step, *thud*. The steps were getting louder and closer.

"Arrr, avast ye matey!" came a yell.

In the doorway stood a life-sized, fully costumed pirate; hook, eyepatch and all. He even had a wooden peg leg, which caused the weird footsteps I'd heard. The guy had spared no expense, everything was top notch, authentic material. Not some mail order Halloween costume, but the real deal.

"Have ye seen me pirate gold, boy?" He flashed his one good eye at me inquisitively as he hobbled closer to my bed. "Have ye seen me pirate gold, boy?"

What the heck was going on? I don't remember ordering the *Pirates of the Caribbean* package when checking into the hospital.

"Who are you and why are you here?" I inquired, trying to get a grasp on what was going on.

"The name's Cap'n Pe'er Malloy," he said, "but you can call me Pirate Pete, if it suits ya." With that he lifted his shiny metallic hook to his brow as though he were giving a salute. "And I travel these halls in search of strapping young lads to sail across the high seas to help me find me gold."

This was a joke, right? One of my friends or family must have sent this guy in a weird attempt to cheer me up.

"So are ye with me, boy," he prodded again. "Will you help me find me gold?"

In spite of myself I let go a small chuckle. As melancholy as I might have been, there was something about this kooky character that just made me smile.

"Well unfortunately, Pirate Pete, I don't think I'll be much help sailing," I finally answered. "Right now, I can't even get out of bed." I patted my legs for good measure.

"Hog Spittle!" he guffawed. "These landlubbers will have you ship-shape before ye can say 'X marks the spot!'"

We talked for a while more and by the end he had me cracking up.

"Do ye know a pirate's favorite letter?" he asked.

I thought for a moment.

"Arrrr," I said in my best pirate voice.

"You'd think that," he said, "but no. Me heart belongs to the 'C!'" He crossed his hand and hook over his chest, looking fondly into space. It was all so absurd. Finally, I could tell the conversation was winding down as he prepared his exit. He grew serious, well, as serious as you can be in a pirate's costume.

"Take it one step at a time, lad." He patted me on the leg for emphasis. "Ye just need one step at a time. But don't waste 'em wandering in the desert. Place your mark and stay true to ye course. You'll find your gold."

And with that, he tipped his ginormous triangular hat, did an about face, and hobbled out of the room. Step, *thud*. Step, *thud*. Step, *thud*. As he left, my wife and the nurse were coming back to the room. He greeted them with a "Ahoy m'ladies!" as they passed each other. Both women entered the room smiling, my wife chuckling.

"Who's that?" she asked.

"Oh, that's CPT Malloy," the nurse responded matter-of-factly. Pointing to the doorway, she added, "He's a hoot, isn't he?"

"Now, when you say 'captain,' what do you mean?" I asked. "I didn't think the Jolly Roger was in port this time of year."

"No, not like that," she chortled at the question. "He's an Army CPT. An O3." Somehow, she knew this didn't get to the heart of the matter, so to stem the flood of questions coming, she went on.

"He came to us about a year ago. While leading his company on a patrol, he was hit by an IED. It really messed him up. Took his leg, hand, and eye. But more than that it took his spirit for a while, ya know? Didn't think he'd ever walk and thought his life was over. It was sad to see. Then one day, one of his buddies visited and brought him a pirate eye patch as a gag and Pirate Pete was born. Before we knew it, he's had the full get up on and was hobbling all over the joint yelling about finding his gold. Now he comes in every once in a while to cheer up our patients. I pray to God I could be half as strong as he's been, ya know?"

I thought about what the nurse had said, trying to envision the goofy looking "Cap'n Pe'er Malloy" as "CPT Malloy," leading his troops in combat. It seemed comical. How on earth did he get from one to the other? Then I remembered the blast, the trauma. It did take a lot of strength to come back from something like that. To look into the abyss of seeming hopelessness and decide to move forward. *One step at a time,* he'd said. *Make my mark and move towards it.*

But what was my mark? I couldn't even get out of bed, let alone search for buried treasure. Still, something about that crazy pirate rang true. If he could do it, I could do it. I might not be dressing up like Jack Sparrow any time soon, but I could get back on my feet. I could find my gold.

After a few more administrative checks, it was time for my surgery. My wife threw down her notepads and folders and wrapped her arms around me in a tight hug, kissed me on the mouth and neck saying, "I love you." Then she pulled away a few inches and looked gravely into my eyes.

"You're going to be okay," she said with deadly seriousness. I saw tears welling up in her eyes. All the emotion she'd been fighting back was finally sneaking through. Her voice cracked as she continued, "But no matter what, I'm here."

With that, she quickly wiped away the single tear which had managed to escape, gave me another short little kiss, cleared her throat, and was back to being the pillar of strength and calm she'd been a moment ago.

"I love you," she said again.

I placed my hand on hers, giving it a small squeeze.

"I love you too, and I'll be okay," as I flashed a sincere smile. Somehow, I knew, everything really would be alright. Even if the surgery didn't go well, even if I never walked again, I had her. Things would be okay. As they wheeled me into the operating room and I laid there, staring up into the bright lights with the oxygen mask now over my mouth, a deep sense of calm washed over me. I really was going to be okay.

Beep, beep, beep.

I woke up back in my room to the familiar rhythmic sound of the heart monitor happily chirping away. I smiled and opened my eyes. Unsurprisingly, my wife was sitting next to me, already holding my hand.

She beckoned the nurse over to let her know the anesthesia was wearing off. Then she leaned in to give me a soft tender kiss.

"I love you, you are okay." It was the last thing she'd said before I went to surgery and the first thing she said when I woke up.

"So how are we feeling?" the nurse asked, interrupting our mini-romantic reunion to check my vitals.

I did a quick internal assessment. I felt good. I was still a bit groggy from the medicine and obviously sore from the surgery, but all-in-all I felt surprisingly good. She moved to the foot of my bed and pulled up the blanket.

"Can you feel this?" she said, poking her pencil into the sole of my foot.

"Ouch!" I startled. Both women traded hopeful, smiling glances.

"That's a good sign," said the nurse. "Now, let's see if we can get you to move your toes."

The following moments were like a scene from the movie *Kill Bill*. With a grin, I repeated the iconic line.

"Wiggle your big toe."

The ladies laughed and then looked down at my feet expectantly. Nothing happened. I searched my mind trying to recall the mind-muscle connection. You don't think about moving, you just move. It's a different feeling and I was out of practice. With Jedi focus, I willed myself into motion. The scientific part of me reasoned, *if you can feel, you can move*. I've got no idea if that's medically sound, but it was all the excuse I needed. My eyes squinted and my brow furrowed as I stared intently down at my lil piggies. Nothing.

Then, a tiny wiggle and at last these lil piggies went "Wee! Wee! Wee!" all the way home. Both my wife and the nurse started freaking out, jumping up and down while hugging. I started laughing like a madman at my toes dancing all around. The food trolley lady heard the commotion and poked her head in to see what was going on and joined in the celebration. Then, overcome by the tidal wave of emotions she'd been holding back, my wife started crying, then the nurse started crying, and even I got choked up. It was beautiful. Amidst the hugging and cheering a thought struck me, a memory. Place my mark and move towards it.

"Quick, grab me pen and paper," I shouted, my voice was excited and urgent.

"Oh, I'm sorry babe, I left my notebook in the car," answered my wife with an apologetic smile. Holy smokes, that thing was basically attached to her, and now in my moment of need it was nowhere to be found. I couldn't help but laugh at the irony. But before I could dismiss the idea, the nurse offered up her pen.

"I've got a napkin you can write on," said the food lady with a shrug. I snatched both, thanking the women, and got straight to pouring my thoughts onto paper before they could fade like mist from my grasp.

Make my mark, I thought. *One step at a time. Just one step.* I let the idea echo in my mind and then scribbled a plan on the napkin. I kept going, building up, increasingly more challenging but still manageable. Walk one mile. Do jumping jacks. More and more. When I'd get stuck or not know how long something might take, I'd ask my wife or the nurse for help. Run one mile without stopping. Do fifty pushups. I kept building up my goals, but I needed something, something big. I needed to place my mark somewhere important that I could drive towards that would keep me motivated when things got tough, something I'd always wanted to do. I needed something my family could be proud of, that I could be proud of. I thought for a moment, chewing on the idea. It seemed crazy, but maybe that's what I needed. With a nod of finality, I wrote in bold thick letters at the bottom of the napkin, *Compete in a bodybuilding competition in 18 months*. With that, I sat back in my bed, staring at the small scrap of thin disposable paper, a smile spread across my face.

"Welp, the hardest part is over. Now I just need to do it all."

The following weeks were hard, but doable. That night, the night after my surgery, I stood up just like I said I would. And the next day, I not only managed to take three steps, but I made it all the way to the bathroom a full day ahead of schedule. One by one, I kept checking off those boxes next to each goal. *Check. Check. Check.*

It was intoxicating. Of course, there were stumbles and roadblocks, but when issues came up or I could see I wasn't progressing towards my goals as quickly as I had anticipated, I would reevaluate.

Was there something I could do to speed up my progress? Was I not pushing myself hard enough? Or maybe I had miscalculated from the start?

There weren't many of those moments, but when they did arise, I talked to my doctors and recalibrated. But man, nothing felt as good as checking off those little boxes. Each seemed so small, so simple, so doable. And yet, one by one, as my list began to fill up with more and more checkmarks, I began to see myself growing closer to the person I was before the injury.

As I followed that progression in my mind, I saw the line of checks, stretching from the devastation of my injury and my utter helplessness, passing through the person I was before the injury, and extending to the person I'd always wanted to be, the man I was meant to be. And as I focused on that image, as I saw that line growing ever clearer, I saw that future me grow more distinct. He was no longer an abstract idea of someone I might be someday, but as real as anything else I'd ever known.

"I'm going to be in a bodybuilding competition," I told the physical therapist as we worked on walking up stairs unassisted.

Sure, I was out of shape and struggling to do more than a few minutes on the step machine; sure I didn't know anything about bodybuilding or have a coach or a competition, but all that would come with time. All I had to do was keep checking off those boxes. And as powerful as those little boxes were, so was my constant proclamations of my ultimate goal.

I told everyone—my family, my friends, the doctors, my coworkers. Heck, even the cashier at the grocery store knew. At first it seemed crazy, but as they started to see how serious I was and how I was progressing, people started cheering me on. Their voices added to the chorus of support pushing me onward. Of course, there were naysayers, there always are. But why should they get the final vote? For each person who besmirched my goals, I had a crowd of people cheering me on.

Take, for example, the first bodybuilding coach I reached out to for help. Let's call him Kenny. It was about a year after the surgery, and I was starting to tiptoe back into the gym in earnest. I'd already come so far, watching my body transform from a feeble, out of shape blob into a run of the mill generally fit dude. I knew I wasn't ready for the stage, but when compared to the major transformation I'd just gone through, it seemed like nothing to do the preparation to compete, the rewarding last leg of an exhausting odyssey when the end is finally in sight. Kenny, however, was unconvinced. He didn't see the hundreds of hours of physical therapy and tortuous exercises. He couldn't see the fire in my eyes or feel the burning determination in my gut, pushing me forward. He just saw an out of shape nobody without any experience.

"Come back once you get a few shows under your belt and then we'll talk," he'd said.

With a smile, I thanked him for his time and left his gym, but I wasn't totally empty-handed. I picked up three things on that visit. First, was a flier for an upcoming natural—steroid-free—competition. It was about six months away and Kenny already had a handful of his regular competitors signed up. I made sure to snag one of the fliers on my way out. Next, was the card of another personal trainer. One of the staff had overheard Kenny's and my conversation and felt bad, so he passed on the info to keep me motivated. This other trainer, Jamie, was new to the scene and dealt mainly with women but might be able to help me. Lastly, I added another goal to my list—prove Kenny wrong.

Jamie was awesome, everything I could have hoped and more. He's one of those genuinely good people who pour themselves out for the benefit of others. When I first met him, he was working out of someone else's gym, set up in a tiny closet in the back. A little sign taped to the door read, "Precision Fitness."

Looking back, I can't help but smile at the memory. In the years since then, from that small, meager beginning, he's since grown his business into a thriving, multi-facility, multi-million dollar fitness center and spa. But even back then, meeting in that tiny closet in a rented out space, I knew he was something special. Not only was he an outstanding coach who knew his stuff, he poured himself fully into his clients. When I first told him my goals, he never once laughed or questioned, he never acted like it was crazy. He just looked me dead in the eyes.

"Let's do it," he said. "I'm with you." And that was that.

Over the next four months, I became obsessed. It was all I thought about. The fear and the doubt, that was gone. I didn't need to think, just execute.

At my left hand was Jamie, knowledgeable and calm, orchestrating all my dietary and exercise needs. Weekly, we'd drive to the city to meet him, and he'd pinch me all over with a caliper to calculate my body-fat. We'd practice posing and he'd give me tips for the next week and then adjust my plan.

At my right hand was my wife, passionate and supportive, helping to prep my meals and pick up slack so I could pursue this dream and heal. I wasn't alone. I wasn't afraid. There were people at my side to help me along and point the way. All I had to do was follow the process and keep checking off tiny boxes—easy.

I'd always wanted to be a bodybuilder, but it had been a "someday" goal. In other words, it's a thing that would be neat, but I have no real plan for how or when—I'd do it someday. But that's just another, less abrupt way of saying never.

"Someday" goals are fantasy; they're pretend, no more real than unicorns or the leprechaun guy on a Lucky Charms box. We need structure. We need a well-defined path with many checkpoints along the way to keep us metered and on track. When we are thrown at giant, seemingly insurmountable problems, it is overwhelming. Instead, we need to segment our goals into small manageable bits. Place your mark and go towards it one step at a time.

So, what's your mark? Is it recovery from an injury? Is it to compete in an athletic event? Or maybe it's to learn a language, or get that special job, or finally break that addiction you know is bringing you down? Whatever it is, place your mark.

Right now, right this very moment, grab a piece of paper, even a napkin if that's all you have, and write down that big mammoth of a goal. I'm not talking about piddly New Year's Eve type stuff, I mean *big*. At the bottom of your paper, write down that crazy huge goal that seems so outrageous you're afraid to even tell it to anyone, for fear they might laugh. That is the goal you want.

Now, make your mark. Working backwards, think of all the things that are needed to build up to that impossibly big goal. Break it into a million tiny pieces, working backwards from big to small, all the way until you get to the seemingly easiest, most benign step. For me, it was "stand up." It doesn't get much more basic than that.

So, you've got a list, but that isn't enough. It might be detailed, but it's still a "someday" goal. You need dates. Next to each of the mini goals, you need to set a time when you'll have the task accomplished. Both the task and the timeframe need to be precise, there can't be any ambiguity whether or not you've completed a goal. Then, once you approach your set date, you need to evaluate.

Did I hit my goal? If not, why?

It's possible you set an unreasonable timeline; you're on the right path and just need a few more days or weeks. It's also possible that you've not been putting in the work and fell behind. But if you never take the time to face that reality and see which circumstance applies, you're never going to grow.

Lastly, that embarrassingly big goal, the one you keep to yourself, you need to tell everyone that you possibly can. Tell your friends and your boss, tell the checkout lady at the grocery store and your barber. Post about it on social media and put notes all around your home. Tell everyone. In doing so, you drive the price of failure up so high that giving up becomes socially untenable. Too often while struggling towards a goal, when we stumble in the brambles and find ourselves lost in the wilderness, we turn around because we think no one is really going to notice. Yeah, you wanted that thing, but oh well. It's hard to push forward and the price for going back is almost nothing. That needs to change.

By binding yourself to those goals and timelines, you make yourself socially accountable to the people in your life. Now there is a cost. If you turn around, everyone will know; so, you keep going. Moreover, those people aren't just watching and judging. Assuming you've surrounded yourself mostly with those who respect and support you, they will almost certainly be cheering you on as you progress. Now, in addition to an accountability structure, you also have a support network to pick you up when you fall.

As I peeked behind the curtain, the bright stage lights blazed down from above. Squinting, I could just make out the outline of my coach in the auditorium. The initial stages of the competition were complete, so he now moved to his seat for the final round of judging. Behind him sat my wife and family who had driven up for the event. My dad was holding up my son, blowing raspberries on his belly to keep him occupied and happy as they waited.

I scanned the large hall, almost every seat was filled, and noticed Kenny. He had brought a handful of bodybuilders who were also competing in this show. I shook off the frustrating memory of our encounter, after all it had led me to Jamie, and focused on the moment. There, at the front of the room, sat the panel of judges.

All that work had led to this—it was time.

They ushered us on stage, all standing in a line. The judges would call out various poses and then make final comparisons as all of us would showcase our physique in the prescribed manner, tensing every muscle in our body while also trying to smile. As we continued to follow direction, flexing and moving about the stage, through the blinding lights, I could barely recognize the silhouettes of my family cheering from their seats. A thought struck me. *I had done it.* Yes, the competition was still ongoing, and I would of course like to do well, but I had completed my goal. From the beginning, the focus was on competing, it was about recovering from this heinous injury and getting to a point where I could step on stage.

That was done. *Check!*

Again, I looked out to see the shadowy figures of my family cheering from the crowd. Thank God for them, and for my coach who took me on even though I was a flabby, injured novice. Thank God for my parents who routinely watched my son and took care of our family when I was training. But most of all, thank God for my amazingly strong wife who was with me every step of the way.

"And now, in first place, please step forward number …"

I heard my number called and my focus snapped back to the moment. Stagehands ushered me to the center of the platform as the auditorium erupted in applause. My family, Jamie, even Kenny stood clapping and cheering. Someone grabbed my wrist and raised it in the air while another draped something heavy around my neck. I looked down to see a gleaming golden medal hanging at my chest. With my free hand, I brought it up to my eyes to admire.

Finally, I'd found my pirate gold.

This event marked one of the greatest triumphs of my life. Not only had I overcome a debilitating injury to compete in a bodybuilding competition, I proved those dirty charlatan naysayers wrong by freaking winning. But it extended even further than that. This victory stretched all the way to my childhood, the climax of a life-long fitness journey designed, in part, to give the middle finger to those shark-eyed boys at the pool. It was then that I began to understand the meaning of *real* victory.

9 ···· TORN FREE

> *"²⁹Then Peter got down out of the boat, walked on the water and came toward Jesus. ³⁰ But when he saw the wind, he was afraid and, beginning to sink, cried out, 'Lord, save me!' ³¹ Immediately Jesus reached out his hand and caught him."* – Matthew 14:29-31

As soon as I walked through the front doors of Fort Leonard Wood's Specker Gym, the familiar sweet stench of steel, perspiration, and excellence filled my nostrils and instantly transported me back to years before. This was the site of my bodybuilding transformation. Nearly a decade prior, I had spent almost every moment of free time within those hallowed walls, sculpting my body and pushing myself further than I had ever gone before. I remembered walking about the gym feeling like an apex predator surveying my domain before demolishing a workout. Other gym goers would look on in astonishment, casting sidelong glances at my physique, further fueling both my ego and motivating me to push harder.

Even then, returning to the site years later while on a business trip, I felt the distant but familiar rumbling as the almost forgotten beast within began to stir.

Bodybuilding had been an incredible chapter in my life. First, acting as a lighthouse, it helped to illuminate my path forward as I overcame the darkness of a debilitating injury. But, having seen some modest success, it became an unquenchable, almost religious cycle of physical self-improvement. A weird combination of constant, narcissistic aggrandizement coupled with body dysmorphia and self-loathing, I was caught between trying to convince myself I was the greatest Adonis to ever walk the face of the earth and feeling like a total fraud. On the best of days, I was somewhere in between these poles. Still, despite the mental turmoil, I look back on that period of my life fondly, recalling the amazing things I was able to accomplish.

Nevertheless, like all good things, that phase of my life had come to an end. After nearly three years of constant dieting and prepping for competition, I decided to switch to powerlifting. Powerlifting was a fabulous alternative. I got to enjoy all the ego-boosting of lifting big-ass weight without that brutal dieting and constant shame of looking in the mirror. Sure, I didn't have a six-pack anymore, but I could put up some ginormous numbers, so I convinced myself it didn't really matter. Plus, it was extremely quantifiable. There were no subjective judges or posing routines, just pure stats. Did my numbers go up? If yes, that was a win. It was awesome and I saw a fair amount of success. During grad school at Yale, I had managed to win the collegiate open for bench press, beating out most of the football team. But even that love faded with time.

As the years progressed, I had become a more active father and role model. Professionally, it was less about my advancement and more about preparing the next generation. My ego and vanity were still there but burned less brightly compared to the richness of everything else. I had found a renewed passion for my faith as I started to let go of the things that had been holding me back. Church wasn't just a Sunday thing, but a daily connection with Christ that filled me with hope and joy. It was a fullness and peace I had never felt before. The "constant pursuit of unattainable perfection" had long since been a part of my mental repertoire, but it was during this time that I began applying the concept to spiritual growth, finding new ways to push myself to be closer to the Lord.

Lent had afforded one such opportunity. Lent is a solemn occasion within the Christian faith, marking the forty days prior to Christ's eventual crucifixion, death and resurrection. Beginning on Ash Wednesday, a time when many Christians mark their head with ashes in the shape of a cross, Lent is supposed to be a time of intense prayer and fasting. Typically, we are called to either give up or add something to our lives that brings us closer to God. In the past, I hadn't necessarily approached Lent with the sincerity that it deserved. But on that occasion, I dove in with vigor and began evaluating my spiritual life in earnest. And I found that one of my stumbling points was how much I had let my fitness slip, letting myself become complacent and lazy. I still lifted of course, by this point in my life moving weight around was a part of my normal existence, kind of like brushing your teeth, but the fire wasn't there. I was simply going through the motions. Importantly, it wasn't my physicality that needed improvement. God doesn't care how much we can lift. Rather, it was my laziness and complacency that needed to change.

There is a connection between the physical and the spiritual, we are both body and soul. Catholics believe that we are divinely crafted in both flesh and spirit, irrevocably entwined and in constant interplay. The spiritual impacts the physical and vice versa. At times, our physical state is a manifestation of our spiritual problems.

In reflection of Lent, thoughts began to echo in my mind as renewed determination and fire spurned me forward to grow both physically and spiritually. *What kind of man are you? What kind of example do you want to set for your boys? How do you react when things are hard? Be the man*

God made you to be. So, in addition to daily prayer and fasting, I also had committed to taking on an intense focus on my weightlifting regimen. Each day I woke early to pray before heading to the gym. It wasn't long before I had started seeing incredible results. I felt amazing. I had a ton of energy and was both fulfilled and happy. I was a more supportive father and loving husband. All aspects of my life began to improve.

And, among these improvements, was my undeniable strength gains. Shortly after Easter, signifying the end of Lent, I entered the 1500-pound club—meaning that my cumulative bench, squat, and deadlift weights totaled more than 1500 pounds. It was a dream come true! Since crossing the lesser 1000-pound threshold at the end of high school, I had been unsuccessfully chasing this new status for many years. Though getting close a few times, I never quite managed to break that barrier. But somehow, without even really intending to do so, I had reached this seemingly unattainable status. It was amazing … and almost by accident. My Lenten goal had been about breaking past my obstacles, but I had been purposeful about not letting physical progress detract from the spiritual. Unexpected, but damn, it had felt good!

Almost overnight, my entire attitude changed. Fueled by vanity, my immense ego had taken over. *If I could get this far by praying, holy smokes, just imagine what I could do if I tried?* In addition to watching my numbers rise, I saw a definite improvement in the mirror. Dormant, forgotten muscles were now bulging from my chest and arms. I also became keenly aware of the growing audience that would form every time I would go to the gym. I wasn't just lifting weights; I was putting on a performance. I had seen my return to Specker Gym as a climax of sorts. Like a fabled hero returned home after slaying a dragon, I had overcome my weaknesses and reemerged even stronger than before.

My first day back, I absolutely obliterated the deadlift and immediately earned my spot on the gym's coveted leaderboard, repping out the previous frontrunner. A small crowd of on-lookers gathered around as I added more and more weight to the bar. From my periphery, I could see people talking and pointing. Their attention just added to the burning fire within. Some of the gym bros, including the guy who had just become second place, came over to make contact. There were a few words of congratulations and shit-talking, high-fives and blustering about the best lifting techniques. It was a language I knew well from years in the "iron jungle." To an alien observer, we must have looked almost indistinguishable from a bunch of howling gorillas in the rainforest, posturing for dominance as they band together. By the end of the workout, we had aligned ourselves, almost like I'd been a part of their little group all along. We agreed to meet back up the following day for chest work.

That day, I entered Specker Gym like a rockstar, doing a lap around the gym before starting my pre-workout routine. I like to start out small and build up, taking my time and savoring the preparation. I hadn't even gotten into my working sets—the heavier, more prescriptive part of my program where I'm actually pushing myself—and people were already starting to watch. I finished the warmup and moved into the heavy sets, systematically hitting my numbers. By this point, the gym bros from yesterday had arrived and were doing their own bench workout on the equipment behind me. This was a good fit. Even though I was there solo, they were close by if I needed a spot.

As I loaded the bar for my last and heaviest set of five, something seemed to take over. My muscles started to quake with anticipation as I loaded the 385 pounds to the bar, which bent slightly under the load. Any sense of restraint people usually showed when covertly watching evaporated completely as they gathered in close to watch and cheer.

"You maxing out, bro?" One guy asked, as he shuffled to the front to get a better view.

"Nope," I responded without looking his way, a hint of annoyance and superiority in my voice.

I sat for a moment on the edge of the bench, breathing in and out deeply as the animal within grew strength. Then, unleashing a roar which mingled with the shout of the crowd, I broke open my smelling salts and inhaled deeply. The intense, harsh smell of the ammonia jolts the system, eliciting a flight-or-fight response and spiking your adrenalin. Immediately, in a flash, everything went dark, and the room was silent as my senses were overcome by the sudden shock of the salts. My pupils shrank to pin pricks and my veins bulged. All that existed in the entire world was the weight and my unyielding rage. Savagely, I threw myself back on the bench and snatched the bar from the restraints.

It felt easy, lighter than it had ever been. First rep—it was nothing. Second rep—this was easy. Third rep—I could do this all day. It felt better than the warmup. As I approached my target rep of five, I started to again hear the cheers of the crowd. People were screaming and jumping up and down. Invigorated, I made a split-second decision to keep going. I gave a quick shout to my spot to let him know I was going to keep going and the gym erupted in applause as I flew past what was supposed to be my final rep.

Easy work, I told myself as I violently spurred my body forward, like a rider trying to push their horse to go faster.

But nothing happened.

I heard a quick intake of breath from the crowd followed by a cry of disgust. For a split-second, I was confused. *What just happened? Why wasn't the bar moving?*

The crowd had seen the damage before I felt it. Then, slightly delayed, the most traumatic and nauseating feeling burst out from within my chest as I both felt and heard meat tearing apart. There was no pain. Perhaps I was in shock or maybe I was still hyped up with adrenaline, but it didn't hurt at first. But with crystal, slow-motion clarity, I sensed as every fiber and sinew of my flesh ripped to shreds and tore away from the bone. The bar hovered in the air for a brief moment before collapsing onto my chest. Thank God for my spotter, who saved me from being totally guillotined.

I rolled away from the bench and stood up. Again, people gasped and jumped away. Through the crowd I caught a glimpse of my reflection in the mirror and understood why. My entire left side hung grotesque and deformed such that I almost didn't recognize myself. What was technically still my arm now draped down the front of my body in an odd, bulging mass. My chest—or what used to be my chest—had somehow disappeared and was now just a sad, sagging purple mass of skin. I stared somewhat quizzically in the mirror, trying to understand what was going on. *Was this really me?*

Apparently, I wasn't the only one disgusted in my new appearance because the guy who had been spotting me promptly vomited on the floor. Everyone else just stared back in horror, too shocked to move. Somehow, I managed to be the most level-headed person in the group.

"You," I shouted, pointing out a random person with my good arm. "Call me an ambulance." I picked out two more, "You guys grab my stuff and help me outside." Then, I added, "And hand me my phone, I need to text my wife."

As they ushered me out of the building, I unlocked my phone to type a quick message to notify my wife. Opening the text screen, amidst the growing haze of agony, I noticed my proceeding text I'd sent less than an hour before. "This is the most excited I have ever been to lift! #EPIC!!!" I shook my head in disgust and disbelief as I recalled all that had happened in such a short amount of time. Epic indeed. How quickly I had fallen, how quickly I'd sank from where I was to this sad monstrosity I had become. But my duties as a husband superseded my embarrassment so I one-handed typed another text to my wife. "Going to ER. I'll be okay. Call when I can." The shock was wearing off and a searing pain was now radiating through my upper body as though I was on fire. I glanced again at those two text messages sent back-to-back. So much had happened between those lines. So much had changed.

At the hospital, I learned I had suffered multiple severe muscle tears. My bicep tendon completely severed and numerous small shoulder muscles detached when my arm dislocated. But most serious was that my left pectoral was destroyed. Unlike my bicep—which had torn free from the bone at the tendon, painful but easily repairable—my pec muscle had been completely ripped to shreds. There was no repairing it, it would need to be removed and replaced with a cadaver transplant known as an allograph.

How many reps had I done? How many pushups and bench press and flies had I performed throughout the years? Certainly, it was in the hundreds of thousands. Maybe even millions. All that work to sculpt and grow, everything I had done to build the oak chest I saw in the magazines. It was all for nothing. It was all gone. That muscle wasn't even physically inside me anymore, thrown in the trash and replaced by whatever they had laying around the morgue.

I'd be lying if I said I wasn't deeply emotionally wounded. For so long, I had used weightlifting as a form of protection. Through my size and strength, I had built up an armor to the world, trying to convince everyone, myself included, that I was impervious to whatever was thrown at me. But over time, I started to forget that the armor was protection and instead was tricked to see it as a part of my identity. So now, with that taken away, it began to feel like I had lost a piece of myself, like a part of me had died. At first, this was deeply troubling. I felt lost and alone, almost betrayed. But through prayer and reflection, I began to understand the truth that had come to pass. Despite my own vanity and pride, I had been gifted a tremendous opportunity.

Since the injury, I often find myself contemplating the story of the disciples witnessing Jesus as he walks on the water. Drawn to the Lord, Peter jumps from the boat and briefly joins Jesus in this seemingly impossible feat. But, as we know, Peter takes his eyes off Christ and becomes consumed with the raging storm around them and promptly sinks. Something about this seemed so unfair. Why would Jesus do that? Why would Christ punish Peter, causing him to fall, just because he looked away? After all, since God is all powerful, He certainly could have kept Peter from plunging into the water if He wanted, right?

Ultimately, I think it is because God gives us what we choose, even when it isn't what He wants. He wants goodness and fullness and joy in our lives, which only comes from union with Him. But, alas, He lets *us* choose our destiny. The more I reflect on that story, the more I believe that Jesus desperately wanted Peter to make it all the way to him, embraced in love and brotherhood atop those waves. Nevertheless, Peter faltered. If only he had trusted. If only he had kept his eyes on the Lord and not let the superficial distractions of the world blind his vision, then I have no doubts that Peter would have stayed dry that day. But he turned away and sank into the depths. And despite this—despite Peter's inability to follow the path God had laid out for him—Jesus still reached into the murky depths to save Peter from himself. His love and power are so great that despite all our failings and bad decisions, God can still raise us from the water to stand with Him.

When I read this story of our brother Peter, I see myself. For the briefest of moments, while truly focusing on the Lord throughout Lent, I was able to accomplish something seemingly impossible in my life. Finally, I felt free of the endless need to impress and prove I was good enough. I was free from the prying, hateful jeers of the shark-eyed boys from my youth, always hiding in the back of my mind to remind me of my shortcomings. I was free to push myself towards a goal, not to impress others, but purely for the sake of struggling to do something great. Like Peter, with my eyes fixed on Jesus, I was able to rise far above anything I could imagine. But then, also like Peter, I became distracted. I averted my gaze and was overwhelmed with vanity and praise. I was once again obsessed with the approval of others, people I didn't even know or really care about.

Instead of serving God, I returned to serving my ego and the materialism of the world. There I stood, at the brink of something amazing, finding a way to achieve the physical excellence I had always wanted without the hang-ups and baggage, but I turned away. And in the blink of an eye, I sank back into the depths. Christ did not cause Peter to sink into the ocean. It was Peter's inability to focus on the Lord that led to failure. Similarly, God did not cause my injury. It was my own hubris and inability to turn from the temptation of vanity. But in both cases, mine and Peter's, despite our failings, God still finds a way to reach into our darkest moments to pull us up and save us. Such is His power and love that He used this massive injury, a disaster of my own making, to tear me free from evil's hold on that part of my life.

God wants us to be strong, but it isn't the physical strength that matters. It is mental and spiritual strength that makes the difference. The physical stuff is just a byproduct. I have no doubts that God would have wanted me to enjoy the frill of weightlifting excellence when done in combination with being the person I was meant to be. But when my vanity stood in the way of my true purpose, He used the natural consequences of my own actions to remove this temptation from my life and bring me closer to Him.

We all let the world deceive us and lead us astray. We are all wandering from the path, blinded by the sparkling trinkets that detract us from our true purpose. But not all that glitters is gold, and such distractions offer no real joy, turning to dust in our hands as we grasp at the grains flowing between our fingers. Life can be hard and none of us escapes without experiencing trauma that weighs us down. The world offers us endless promises to lighten our load—social media and movies, commercials and materialism, medications and magic treatments. So many of us become engrossed in the splendor of these false idols that we lose sight of where we are meant to go, who we ought to be. But these are pale substitutes for real salvation—sour vinegar in place of sweet wine. Such distractions are waves, crashing against us, drawing our attention away from the light and threatening to bring us down. We find ourselves pursuing goals, not for righteousness but for praise, only to feed into our growing brokenness. Thus, we sink deeper, seemingly caught in an endless cycle, unable to escape.

However, there is a way out of this hellish loop. There is hope and greatness in store for us. All we have to do is let go and tear ourselves free from the bonds of this world that hold us back and fulfill our purpose. Don't be the person others want you to be. Don't even try to be the person *you* want to be. Instead, strive to be the person you *ought* to be. Achieve the purpose God made you for. You should absolutely pursue greatness, but not for the glory. Rather, you should pursue it for *The Glory*. Do it because the struggle brings you closer to knowing Christ and shining His light through your life.

I'll be honest, I'm still not completely physically recovered from the injury. I'm fit and I'm improving. There's been a mountain of physical therapy and the doctors are monitoring my progress with expert care. I'm motivated and getting stronger every day, but I will never be the same. If I could snap my fingers and be as strong as I was before, I'm not sure that is what I would want. There's nothing to prove anymore. I don't *need* to be that guy. Yes, of course, I want to be as physically fit as possible to better perform my duties as a soldier. But let's be honest, there was never going to be a time when I needed to bench press a tank. I wasn't doing that for the Army, I was doing it for me—for my ego.

But now that's gone, and now I care about fulfilling my duties as a professional as well as a husband and father. I care about exercising both my body and my spirit as I push towards greatness in a much more well-rounded fashion. I'm able to let go of all that garbage from before, excising the demons that had haunted me for so long.

Look within. Understand how the trauma and pain of your past has marred you, bumping you from the path you were meant to walk. Identify what baggage you are still carrying. Then, let it go. Loosen your clenched fists from around that memory you are holding onto for dear life, and it will release its hold over you. Gaze upon yourself in the mirror—scars and all—without the burden of your past and appreciate how you have been designed by the Creator for something truly special. These scars and blunders are a part of the crucible of life that has forged you into a strong and capable leader. Leverage your past to drive you towards success, not to appease others, but because it is what you were made for.

As I look back, I recognize that a huge part of my physical identity was tied to some stupid silly shit from my childhood. When the sting had worn off, the scar had remained and affected my thoughts and actions. Even the bodybuilding and weight training were tied to that moment as part of my endless endeavors to prove them wrong. It wasn't for me really—not entirely—it was for them. To show them how much they didn't matter. Which, ironically, proved more than anything how much they *did* still have a hold on my life. It was only after I suffered the injury—only after I was torn away from that temptation—that I finally found freedom.

.... PART THREE: GOLDEN NUGGETS FOR SUCCESS

10 ···· CAPTAIN PLANET

"If words of command are not clear and distinct, if orders are not thoroughly understood, then the general is to blame." – Sun Tsu

There is an old expression that was drilled into my head during my early years of officer training. The adage states that, "a leader is responsible for everything that does and doesn't happen within their organization." I heard this many times throughout my basic officer training, but, like many young officers, I didn't fully buy into the concept. Deep down I felt this was a gross oversimplification and frankly, a bit unfair, if not absurd.

Take, for example, the beloved fictional character of Private Snuffy known to all Army leaders. If PVT Snuffy got drunk and got into a fight at the bar, was that my fault? Was it because I, his fictional platoon leader, had not properly impressed the importance of the Army values? Or was it because I hadn't provided a thorough enough safety-briefing at the end of the week? If only I had spent a few more minutes precisely detailing the circumstances of every possible situation he would encounter and the correct choices in each, perhaps he might have known what to do. Or maybe—and this is a radical idea—people could be responsible for their own actions.

Also, how high up does this principle go? So, PVT Snuffy does something bad. At what level should his leadership be reprimanded? Obviously, the platoon leader. Bring out the torches and pitch forks. But what about the company commander? The battalion commander? The brigade? At what point do we haul the commanding general out of his fancy office and wag our finger in his face because of what PVT Snuffy did?

Well, truthfully, that all depends on how bad of a thing ole Snuffy was up to. There have been a few rare occasions when top brass got *shwacked* for something that happened in their ranks, but they are always for something extreme. In my experience, the majority of these things tend to isolate themselves down to the lower levels. So, like it or not, I repeated back the old phrase about leaders and our omniscient responsibilities and accepted this as part of the job. After all, that's why we get paid the "big bucks," as they say. It wasn't until I arrived to my first unit that I began to understand. Through an unfortunate series of events midway through my time as a platoon leader, I enjoyed the exciting opportunity—which is another way of saying it was terrible, but I survived—of learning the finer points of that old adage.

That exciting opportunity was *Prop Blast*.

We were on day two of our little adventure and had already walked nearly thirty miles. The bright green mullet wig now looked muddy brown and large patches were glued to my face with sweat. Most of the blue body paint that covered my face and hands was cracked and faded, and the spandex superhero outfit was covered in mud. I looked less like my assigned role as Captain Planet and more like a giant hobo Smurf. As we crested the next hill, we found our "Blaster" standing in a clearing with his clipboard. Behind him loomed yet another set of obstacles.

"Alright, Blastees," he bellowed. "You've got ten minutes to hydrate before completing this station!"

With groans of both pain and relief, we threw our gear to the ground and collapsed. No one had gotten more than a few hours of sleep and we were running on fumes, but the end was in sight. Searching for my canteen in my ruck, I pushed aside the giant bag of "grass seed"—which was really a sandbag. I had been gifted the large sack the day prior and required to lug around since. Around me, others pulled out their own equally ridiculous "gifts." One guy was given several two-liters of soda to commemorate him spilling his drink on the battalion rug. Another guy wore a tight, pale night gown or "white slip" as a reminder that he had refused to test for his jumpmaster white slip. It was all shenanigans.

"Captain Planet!" the Blaster shouted. "Don't worry about that canteen. I've got another present for you."

I hopped to my feet and rushed over with all the enthusiasm I could muster as the voice in my head let out a groan. I knew it wasn't anything good. Approaching my Blaster, who was actually a good friend of mine, I rendered a salute and gave my official greeting for what must have been the thousandth time. I threw my fist in the air and shouted Captain Planet's famous catchphrase, "with our powers combined, I am Captain Planet!"

This was one of the rules. Every time you got called by one of the Blasters, you had to report using your assigned greeting. With a chuckle, my Blaster handed over a full gallon jug of water. Written in big black marker were the words "Tears of the Environmentalists."

"Drink up, buddy," he said with a sardonic grin as he patted me on the back.

Yes, this was Prop Blast. It is a standard "team building" event done in most airborne units to welcome new officers. The entomology for the event is unique. When you jump out of a plane during an airborne operation, you are hit by a violent blast of air created from the plane's propeller systems. This gust of air is known as the prop blast. The whirlwind experience is where that fun event I was participating in derived its title. Each new officer going through the event (aka Blastee) is assigned a seasoned officer (aka Blaster) to watch over them throughout all the festivities. Each Blaster gives a unique name to their Blastee and grants various items as "gifts" of personal meaning. Don't get me wrong, it totally sucked but it was all in good fun and was much more about welcoming cherished teammates than about just screwing with people. Looking back, it ranks highly among my most cherished memories in the airborne community.

My Blaster's name was Jake. He was a good buddy of mine, which is probably why he took so much pleasure in messing with me. Shaking my head, I ripped the jug out of his hands and took a sip. But before I could swallow, the taste hit me, and I spat the liquid to the ground.

"It's salty!" I exclaimed in bemused wonder. Jake stared back.

"Yeah man, they're supposed to be tears, and tears are salty," he said flatly. "Besides, electrolytes are good for you. Drink up!" he added as he gestured for me to raise the jug to my lips.

It reminded me of the exceptionally gross CeraSport packets they made us drink at airborne school, but at least those had a little bit of flavoring. I looked back at the jug and shook my head in resignation.

"Screw you, dude," I laughed and then started to chug, in a vain attempt to drink the whole thing.

How had I gotten myself into all of this?

As soon as I thought it, it came back to me. A few months prior, about midway through my platoon leader time, things were going well. My platoon sergeant and I had built a solid team from scratch. We prided ourselves on being the highest performing construction platoon in the entire brigade. Through countless training events we had cultivated a well-oiled machine capable of accomplishing whatever was thrown our way. If there was some high priority or last-minute project, you could bet we were the ones called to get the job done.

Around this time, our battalion was conducting Sapper Stakes. This once-a-year competition focused on assessing individual squads as they completed a series of military exercises. In preparation for this year's event, our platoon was charged with construction of a small obstacle course. The location, however, had not yet been determined. Nevertheless, we were assured it would be in a field somewhere. So right away we set to work on developing a plan, building obstacles, and prepping all the necessary resources.

Finally, after weeks of work, the plan was complete, and everything was ready. We just needed a location to set up. With some prodding, we were able to get the battalion staff to provide us an eight-digit grid for where they wanted us. On the map, it appeared to be a large field about a half-hour away. Like any bright, young lieutenant, I immediately set out to do a leader recon. We loaded up the trucks and headed off to inspect our future jobsite. But when we arrived, we did not find a field. Instead, we found a grove of small ten-foot pine trees amidst the forest of larger, more established foliage.

Obviously, this was not going to work. Besides the fact we had planned a bunch of running-around-in-a-field type activities, I'd been near construction enough to know you can't just set up shop in the middle of the woods without having to chop through a proverbial forest of red tape first. So, I rushed back to explain the situation and request a different location. Unfortunately, the staff officer running the show—a self-superior, slightly higher ranking first lieutenant—was a bit of a hard-ass.

"Negative, second lieutenant," was the response. "You're just going to have to figure it out."

After a bit more digging, I was able to get confirmation that if we didn't mess with the trees, we would be fine.

Coincidently, it was also at this time that my platoon sergeant and I learned we were being sent on a last-minute trip for a week to attend a construction conference, so I rallied my squad leaders to discuss the plan in our absence. We would be gone for the remaining preparation for Sapper Stakes, so it was up to them to emplace all the obstacles. Placing my most senior squad leader in charge, I informed them of the changes to our original plan.

"FRAGO," I told the team.

FRAGO, short for Fragmentation Order, is a standard term used to describe when you adjust or add to an existing plan. Unconsciously, they pulled out their leader books and prepared to write down the changes.

"We're going to have to scrap a lot of the stuff because of all the trees. Don't worry about any of the races they were going to do in the field. Instead, just place the obstacles a little bit off the firebreaks so they don't mess with any of the vegetation."

My squad leaders confirmed their understanding of the new plan, and we headed out. The week went by without any issues. My platoon sergeant and I might have been gone, but I wasn't worried. We had an exceptional team and I had no doubts in their ability to accomplish the mission. Of course, we called back to check in on the platoon's progress, but as expected they assured us everything had gone smoothly. When we returned, the whole platoon was ecstatic to show off all their hard work. Almost immediately, we hopped in the trucks and headed out to inspect the fruits of their labor.

"You're going to love it, sir," assured the head squad leader. "We went all out on this one. The guys pulled a few late nights, but we really wanted to knock this out of the park for you!"

Moving the obstacles was a decent sized job but it should not have taken that much time. Why would they need to pull an all-nighter? Something about it didn't sit well with me but I kept smiling and said I looked forward to seeing their work.

"You can always count on us to get the job done," he continued. "You both worked so hard on that original plan. It would have been such a shame for your hard work to go to waste. So, we took care of it."

Took care of it. The phrase rattled around in my brain for a few moments. *What the hell did that mean?*

But before I could put the pieces together, we turned into the site and my jaw dropped. I looked over at my platoon sergeant, who seemed to echo my emotions—his mouth bobbing up and down like a fish gasping for air as he tried to form words. Jumping out of the truck, my squad leader threw up his arms in a *ta-da* motion and gestured to the open space behind him, like he was unveiling a prize.

It was a complete disaster. There wasn't a single tree for as far as you could see—the dense forest had been leveled to a parking lot. I have seen deserts with more vegetation. Looking out over the barren wasteland, the magnitude of the situation began to sink in.

We were totally screwed. Correction. *I* was totally screwed. An officer is responsible for everything their unit does or fails to do. It seemed immensely unfair at the time, but, as I would later come to accept that this was my fault. I may have told my squad leader to not mess with the trees, but I hadn't really explained how important it was. To me it was obvious, but I was the one who always dealt with the construction permits. For a young NCO, their focus is on getting the mission done. In the absence of clear intent, they thought they were doing the right thing.

There was no getting around it; I owned this shit sandwich. I looked up at the guys. They beamed back at me, smiling from ear to ear with pride in what they believed to be a job well done. And in truth, it was pretty amazing. But I was still completely hosed. In an effort to please me, they had gone way above and beyond anything I would have imagined. Despite the soul-crushing realization that I would more than likely be fired for this incredible mistake, a small part of me managed to feel grateful for their dedication. I pulled my phone out and looked to my platoon sergeant, who shot back a knowing glance.

"Make the call," he said solemnly and then pulled the other NCOs together to explain the situation. I stood for a full minute just staring at the number pulled up on my phone steeling myself for the inevitable ass chewing. Then I took a big breath and called my battalion commander.

Many officers spend their whole careers afraid of messing up, so they don't do anything of importance and, when problems inexorably occur, they try passing the blame onto someone else. The first makes them a coward, but the second makes them a dishonorable coward. Own your mistakes. They aren't failures, they are opportunities for growth. Push yourself. Push your team. Maybe you truly are that one in a billion all-star who gets everything right all the time. But I guarantee that's not the case for your subordinates. If you're lording over them all the time, they're never going to grow. Give them space to make mistakes and provide them top cover.

Take risks, *prudent* risks. Mitigate what you can, have a plan for the rest, and move out. Don't spend your life cowering in the corner, too afraid of stubbing your toe that you never do anything awesome. Step into the arena and swing for the fences. If you miss, then learn, recalibrate, and keep swinging. But with that, you also must be okay with the consequences when things don't go your way, because *you* are responsible for everything your unit does or fails to do. Like it or not, you are the one on the line, so you need to be willing to pay the price. For example, you unequivocally should be giving your NCOs the authority to accomplish the mission without you micromanaging every moment of their lives. But also appreciate that if you happen to not fully understand their capabilities and mindset, and then give them a mission without clearly articulating their left and right limits, and they mistakenly deforest a wildlife preserve … well, my friend, you've got to be ready to get your ass chewed. Or maybe worse.

And oh, I definitely got my ass chewed. First by my commander, then by range control. By the end of it, the Environmental Protection Agency had showed up and we spent the next several weeks planting trees and spreading grass seed. But to my total amazement, I was not relieved of my position. Instead, after his initial fire and fury, my commander pulled me into his office and talked with me man to man. He listened to my story and taught me "the mirror test." Whenever something doesn't go your way, look in the mirror first, and ask what you could have done to achieve a different result. Even if you don't think it is your fault, you still have to look in the mirror. Because at the end of the day, the only thing you can really change are your own actions. I might not have even been in the state at the time my guys were sawin' pine, but I could have identified the risk and better communicated such action was unacceptable. Luckily for me, just as I had backed my squad leader, I had a commander who cared enough to support and mentor me.

"We all make mistakes," he said with a pat on the back. "Hell, if I told you the shit I got into as an LT, you'd probably request a transfer. Shake it off and get back in the fight."

I thanked him and started to walk towards the door.

"One last thing before you go," he said as he shot me a stern look that sucked the air out of the room. "If anything like this ever happens again, anything at all, it's lights out. Tracking?"

"Tracking, Sir."

"Good! Besides," he smiled, "maybe something good will come of this. Prop Blast is coming up and it occurred to me that you'll need a name." His smile grew even wider. "I think Captain Planet will do quite nicely."

As a leader, you are endowed with immense responsibility. Never forget this sacred duty to the unit and to your soldiers. But this is just one side of the coin. With responsibility comes authority. So often power turns men into tyrants and we try to ignore the innate authority of command. But when approached with humility, understanding this aspect of leadership can help you to be a more adept teammate, whether you are in a leadership or subordinate position. Appreciate your role and where you exist within this power structure.

11 ···· "THE WALL" TEST

"Who is your daddy, and what does he do?" – Arnold
Schwarzenegger, *Kindergarten Cop*

"Sir, I just don't think he's going to let us do that."

My company commanding officer's (CO) eyes widened as his head jerked back with a combination of surprise and disgust. But the reaction was not from the news. It was the way I said it.

"*Let* us?" he repeated, drawing out each word and letting them hang in the air like a question.

We had been going back and forth with the battalion executive officer (XO) for a few days about moving our shipping containers from the staging area. The CO wanted them closer to our building for easier access, but the XO kept refusing because he wanted all battalion equipment consolidated. This argument had been raging for a few days, with me acting as their little messenger boy, constantly running between them to mediate. In truth, the argument wasn't really about shipping containers.

143

Deep down at the core it was about power and control. The whole thing with the equipment location was just a proxy war, one of the many battles in their constant vying for control to see who's thing (and by *thing*, I mean sphere of influence) was bigger.

The CO wasn't shocked to learn about the XO's opposition to moving our equipment closer to the building. Of course, he opposed it. Anything the CO wanted, the XO would have opposed, and he was upset I would dare to infer that the XO might have the authority to make a decision over him. At that time, I was also an XO, but at the company level. XOs are supposed to handle all of the operational activities in their organization, as they run the staff—supply acquisitions, operations, maintenance, medical, and the like. The CO gets to make decisions while the XO tries to scramble to figure out how to make it work. Having been both, serving as a commander is amazing. Conversely, serving as an XO is tireless, thankless, and often frustrating work. It is also probably the most important developmental position you will experience, as you prepare to take command.

The relationship between the company CO and company XO is well-defined. The CO is the boss and the XO works for him. Technically, an XO's job is to run the staff, but a well-known truth is that the XO's real job is to do whatever tasks the commander doesn't want. Like Dwight Schrute from *The Office*, you're the assistant to the regional manager. However, my understanding of how the company interfaced with the battalion XO was more ambiguous. After all, the battalion is at a higher level than the company, and its XO is at the rank of a Major—higher than the typical CO rank of a Captain. So, in my eyes, the Battalion XO seemed to be on sure footing.

"Sir, I'll ask again if you want, but he seems to have made up his mind. I just don't think he's going to change his decision."

"Decision?" the CO balked.

"Decision!" he bellowed loudly, for a second time. "Fine! Let's take it to 'The Wall.'"

He jumped up from his desk and began briskly striding towards the front of our company so quickly I had to run to keep up. Over his shoulder I could hear him muttering and grumbling something about "the chain of command ... the chain of *command*."

We finally stopped in front of the decorative wall covered in framed photographs of well-dressed military men looking sternly into the camera. Commonplace in most military organizations, this type of wall displays the photos of the leaders at every organizational level. On the far left was CO's familiar grim face. To his right hung images of similar-looking shorthaired, steely-eyed men who became progressively older the higher their position. As I moved further to the right, the men were not wearing uniforms at all, but sharp-looking suits with American flag pins on their lapels. I could not help but notice that the higher in position, the more they smiled in their photo. Filing the epiphany away for another time, I turned back to my CO.

"Do you know what this is?" he barked, pointing to "The Wall."

It wasn't my first day in the Army, so of course I knew.

"Yes, sir," I answered.

He stared back blankly, moving his arm in a revolving "go on" motion as though my response did not provide the appropriate explanation. This was ridiculous. Of course, I knew what the photos were. And he knew that I knew. Hell, I was the one who hung the photos on "The Wall" in the first place. It wasn't about that; he was angry about feeling outdone by the XO and wanted to show how in charge he really was. I played his stupid game.

"These are the photos of our chain-of-command." I stood up a bit taller, stared him dead in the eyes, and tried to speak as clearly as possible.

Obviously, I'd pissed him off with my earlier comment and now he was making me go through this charade to prove a point. Still, if I'm going to take one on the chin, you can bet I'm going to be standing tall like a grown-ass man.

"The chain of *command*," he repeated, again emphasizing the last word. "And who are the people who make decisions?" he asked rhetorically, rubbing his chin and pretending to be deep in thought. "Hmmmmm, who could it be?"

He tapped his index finger against his chin a few times for greater emphasis. The question hung in the air for a few moments. Finally realizing he wanted me to answer.

"Commanders, sir," I responded flatly.

He threw his hand in the air, pointing to the sky as if we had discovered some long-plaguing mystery.

"Commanders!" he exclaimed. You could see he was proud of himself. He'd written some absurd play in his mind to teach me a lesson and we were acting it out perfectly.

"Wait, but now I'm confused," he continued, now taking on an air of faux bewilderment. "I don't see the Battalion XO up there. You said these are the commanders and that commanders are the ones that make decisions, but where is he?" He started to point at the photos again.

"There's me, and there's the battalion commander, and over there is the brigade commander. Oh, and look, over there is the President."

He turned back around to look me in the eye.

"But wait. Did I miss something? Where is he?"

I sighed a deep breath. Gosh, I hated this guy.

"He's not there, sir," I replied, sheepishly.

"Aahhh, yes. He's *not* up there." The fake jovial tone now left his voice completely. "And that must mean that he doesn't make decisions, does he?" He was shouting now, wrapped up in a frenzy, his ultimate point resulting in a crescendo.

"But I'll tell you who does. *Me*."

Now his voice dropped suddenly to almost a whisper, and he took a step closer until his face was inches from my own.

"Move. The. Container," he said crisply, articulating every word and then walked away.

I stood there for a bit staring at those photographs on "The Wall," chewing on everything that had just happened. *What was my next move?* I liked the XO. He was a good guy. He was smart, hardworking, and went out of his way to mentor me and the other company XOs on how to do various staffing duties. On the other hand, I thought my CO was a pompous ass who seemed to get away with anything. He was brash and more than a little drunk with power. But at the same time, he wasn't a complete idiot and he worked hard to move us in what he saw as a positive direction. *So, what to do?*

If the question was "who would I rather grab a beer with?" the answer would have been easy—the XO, obviously. But this was different. This was a question of who to follow. Looking up at those photos, I reviewed the standard mental checklist of times when it is acceptable not to follow an order. Nothing about what the CO said was immoral, unethical, or illegal so I had no recourse for disobeying. Then again, the same could be said about what the XO told us to do. *So, which one to choose?*

I looked back at the wall of sharply dressed leaders staring back at me. Their stern, judging eyes pierced through me as if to say, "Choose wisely." Most of all was the CO. But one face was missing from "The Wall," someone who at this moment in time didn't warrant the place of honor among the wall of commanders. So, I made my decision.

By the end of the day, two things happened: the shipping containers were moved next to our building and the Battalion XO was throwing an absolute shit fit in front of your company area. He must have heard the shrill *beep* of the forklift as it backed the container into place. And like a racehorse breaking free from the starting gate, XO burst from the battalion offices and sprinted towards us. His eyes were frenzied and full of rage.

Saliva spewed from his mouth as he screamed a torrent of unintelligible curses in our direction. I had suspected something like this, although not to this magnitude, might transpire so I made a point of being outside to provide cover for the forklift operator.

I watched as the XO shot towards us, closing the distance faster than I would have imagined. He wasn't running, he was sprinting. For a moment, I thought he might actually run me over and I instinctively braced for impact. But then, in the last instance, he pulled up short. Incensed, he wagged his trembling finger in my face as he continued to shout. Amidst the cacophony of curses and momentary gasps for breath, I could make out fragments of barely formed visceral thoughts as they tumbled over each other to escape his lips.

"But you can't … I said that you ... How dare he … I'm gonna crush his …"

It went on like that for a while, him shouting and wagging his finger. I raised my hands and gave a reproachful look as if to say, "It's not me, dude. Just following orders." A small part of him relented and he dropped his hand. He knew it wasn't my fault. After all, I was just doing what my boss told me and, as he knew, *he* wasn't my boss. He turned away from me and aimed his ire toward the container itself as if the slow movement of the steel box were symbolic of his own inexorable loss of control. Again, he started shouting and cursing, pulling his hair and beating his chest. At one point he even jumped up and down like a little child protesting their mommy's decision to take their toy. It was sad to see a man at such a low point, especially since he was someone I generally respected. But for these short moments, the man had cracked, and his pure uncontrolled emotion was escaping out the fissure like a geyser.

I'm confident he would have recovered. The tantrum would have run its course and he would have regained his composure and seen how his behavior was inappropriate. He would have apologized and found a professional, diplomatic and level-headed way of dealing with the situation, but he never got the chance. Right as he was jumping up and down like a petulant child, pulling out his hair and cursing into the wind, our CO walked out the front door of our building shoulder to shoulder with the Battalion Commander.

As it turns out, earlier that day, following my oh-so-fun introduction to "The Wall," our CO invited the Battalion Commander over to the company to check out some new supplies. They got to chatting and telling old war stories. CO was always good at rubbing elbows and used it to his benefit.   Somewhere along the way, he casually slipped in how vital it was to have our container close to the building so we would be moving it sometime today.

"Seems reasonable to me," the Battalion Commander had replied nonplused. It was the first he had heard of the issue and was completely unaware of the ongoing feud between my CO and the XO. In his mind, if one of his company commanders thought it was a good idea, why should he stand in their way?

"Let the XO know if there's anything the battalion can do to help."

With that, CO nonchalantly transitioned to the next story and the whole issue was settled. He had the backing of the Battalion Commander—the guy, the head cheese, the old man. Someone above him on "The Wall" said it was okay, which made it a done deal. The two of them wrapped up the rest of their business and headed out the door to continue their fine airborne day. Well, that was until they came outside and found the Battalion XO throwing a fit.

"What in the hell is going on here?" demanded the Battalion Commander. XO spun around to find his boss glaring accusatorially at him. His head darted back and forth trying to understand what was happening as he stammered.

"I … I … I was, ahhhh …" A mixture of fear and embarrassment washed over his face as he began to understand the situation.

"This is outrageous!" the Battalion Commander continued. "Report to my office immediately."

And that was the end of that. My CO got his container moved, the Battalion XO got an official reprimand, and I learned a valuable lesson: know who your boss is.

Look, you aren't always going to like your boss. They might be dramatic or condescending, they might micromanage or be a bit of a dummy. For the most part, I've been pretty fortunate with having excellent leadership. But they aren't all God's gift to the world and occasionally you get a burnt potato chip out of the bag.

Stand up for what you think is right and voice your opinion. Regardless—whether you love your boss with every fiber of your being or go to bed each night praying they fall down a well—you've got to know who your boss is. Who is the dude or dudette signing your evaluation? Don't compromise your values just to get good paper, that's not what I'm saying. Obviously, if your boss is genuinely doing something unacceptable, don't just go along with it. If atrocities like My Lai and Abu Ghraib taught us anything, it's that we need soldiers strong enough to stand up to injustice, even when it's hard. That's not what I'm talking about here, though. I'm talking about the other 99.9 percent of the time when your boss isn't doing something illegal, unethical, or immoral; they're just doing something you don't like. Those are the times when you need to take a big ole' cup of suck-it-up juice and get the job done. It might be frustrating, and I hope you get a new boss soon. But right now, it's their world, you're just living in it.

On the upside, the Army moves you so much that one of you is inevitably leaving in the near future. One day, much sooner than you might think, you are going to be a commander. When such a day comes, you need to understand the full weight of what the moment really means and all the power and responsibility that comes with the position. What's that thing Spiderman is always saying?

"With great power comes ..." you know the rest.

You've got to understand both sides of that coin—power and responsibility. The latter of these is often beat into our heads as young officers, but the idea of understanding your power seems taboo. However, having an appreciation for the intrinsic authority wielded in this position doesn't necessarily mean you are a self-indulging tyrant—although we've all met plenty of those. By respecting the immense power that is bestowed on that position, if done with humility and reverence, you can gain an even deeper appreciation for the sacred charge of command.

The Army is a team sport, which can be a tremendous benefit. I've been saved more times than I can count by the wisdom of those at my side. But also understand that amidst the chorus of voices, shouting advice and tugging an organization in a thousand different directions, it's ultimately up to the commander to chart the path forward. For now, as you wait for your turn in the hot seat, don't just sit back judgmentally, whispering to your friends about what a better job you could have done. Instead, be the person you wish was supporting you if you were the one in charge. Speak your mind behind closed doors and then be their fiercest advocate going forward. And one day, when you finally are the one with your name on the building, take up the mantle with humility, respecting both your power and your responsibility.

Like the famous quote from C.S. Lewis says, "Humility is not thinking less of yourself; it is thinking of yourself less." Don't ignore the authority briefly granted to you; rather, exercise it masterfully to the benefit of your organization. Surround yourself with advisors, wise and experienced. Block out the noise of haters and naysayers as best you can. But if those negative voices grow too loud, or you ever doubt what you can do or who you should listen to ... take it to "The Wall."

Learning how to appropriately wield authority as a humble servant leader is only one aspect of appreciating the complex topology of leadership. An equally effective tool is understanding how to leverage the power of perception. As you'll see, some use this tool nefariously for selfish, self-aggrandizing reasons. However, like any tool, it is possible to brandish such capability to better serve your unit and communicate the excellent work of your soldiers.

12 ···· MAKE IT GREEN

"Perception is more important than reality. If someone perceives something to be true, it is more important than if it is in fact true." – Ivanka Trump

Once upon a time ... I detested my boss.

Let's call him Chad. Chad was perfect. Well, no; actually, he was a lying sack of crap. But on paper, he seemed like God's gift to the world and all the top brass loved him. As they say, he was all *show* and no *go*.

Chad wasn't sadistic or overly aggressive. He never even really yelled. In fact, I think I would have liked him more if he had raised his voice every once in a while. At least that would have shown a little emotion. I had spent the better part of my life playing sports and I was more than accustomed to a good ass-chewing now and again. But that was not Chad's style. It would have made him too real, too human. He was more like a robot with only one setting—insincere politeness.

And so, all the guys in the unit detested him too.

Like one of those cheap freeze pops they give out at kids' parties, Chad was so sickeningly sweet and utterly fake; a paper cutout of a politician. It was like everything he said was being read from a teleprompter; checking off the boxes on some "how to be a good leader and say the right thing" list. Chad was always shaking hands, always smiling. After lunch each day he would walk around the unit telling people what a valued member of the team they were, but you could tell it was total bullshit. It was almost comical to watch him unenthusiastically feign conversation with the soldiers.

"How are we doing, men?" he would shout to no one in particular, as he breezed past—not even listening for a response. There might as well not have been anyone in the room. "Mmmm, yes. Very good, very good. Well, keep up the great work."

On the rare occasion someone was able to pierce through his never-ending torrent of platitudes to engage him in real conversation, Chad would awkwardly mumble phrases like "I see …" or "we'll look into that," until he was able to break away. It was obvious that he didn't value us— we were just a means to an end, which made it worse than if he just stayed in his office and not visited at all. It was infuriating. You wanted to shake the guy to make him say something, *anything* authentic.

Perhaps the most unique of Chad's insincere behaviors was a strange conversational tic he had developed. Every single interaction he had with someone, no matter the content or length of the conversation, would always end with him saying "thanks, man." It was so ridiculous it became funny. So of course, we turned this into a game. The goal was to get Chad to say those magic words as many times as you could during one interaction. We even had a little whiteboard outside of his office where we kept score (the highest score was twelve times in a single conversation).

Was this stupid and petty and immature?

Yeah, of course.

But in our defense, we never involved any of the enlisted guys in the game. That would have been over the line, even for us. Besides, they probably had their own, much more inappropriate game to keep them occupied. Anyway, it helped us relieve some of the stress of working for the guy.

So, why did we detest the guy so much?

Yeah, Chad was kind of lazy and not super competent, but there were lots of people like that. I guess it was because he was so inauthentic. This guy was a hypocrite and it drove us nuts. Chad said all the "right" words, but he never actually lived up to them. Often, he would come to work late or skip out on training altogether. Well, that is, unless his leadership was coming by. In that case, he would rush to the action to seem like he was really "leading from the front." We could always tell if someone important was scheduled to visit, because Chad would be standing tall and giving commands like he was General Patton. To us, it seemed so obvious that Chad was a buffoon and we were the ones keeping the organization afloat. Not *because* of him, but *in spite* of him. We kept expecting the leadership to finally see through the bullshit, but somehow, they never caught on.

But despite all Chad's shortcomings, despite his almost complete lack of tactical knowledge or work ethic, despite everything, the man had an astounding ability to make himself look good to his superiors. More than anyone I have ever met, Chad understood precisely what was needed to create the perception in the mind of the leadership that he was a high performer. It was absolutely mystifying. He would miss a full day of training and then miraculously appear for ten minutes during a photo-op. Every storyboard we sent up had to include a picture of him making commanding gestures to "his troops." And, above all else, every single tracker had to have a "green status."

Always, *always* green.

The Army loves trackers. As the name suggests, they are used to "track" the status of anything from personnel statistics to mission completion. Often, especially in larger organizations, these trackers can become rather lengthy and cumbersome. To help commanders digest this information quickly, we use a red / amber / green system to provide immediate visual feedback as to the status of the task. Red indicates a task that has not been started or has a major issue, amber is for tasks that are being worked on but are not complete, and green is used for completed tasks or when there are no issues. Those colors are powerful. Red makes commanders unhappy, but green makes the boss smile. And Chad understood this.

How's the maintenance status? Green.

Did you do all that training? Yep, we are "green."

What about that tasking that came out last night that you could not possibly have had time to finish? Like Kermit the Frog eating a sack of limes on St. Patrick's Day, you could bet, we're "green" on that too!

Often this was at the expense of the soldiers. There are many times in the military when you must buckle down and stay late for the sake of the mission. That's fine, we all knew what we signed up for when we joined the Army, but this was not that. Chad didn't care about the mission. He simply cared about the color of his slides; he cared about *him* looking good. So, all of us in the unit would pay the price for his insane desire to needlessly rush to push through a tasking weeks ahead of the due date, just so he could brief a green status. And if it wasn't physically possible for us to be done in time for the meeting, Chad would do some "hand waving" and make the slides green anyway.

Finally, I'd had enough.

Every year, units prepare a briefing to their higher headquarters detailing their status on a variety of training events. We had done exceptionally well and prided ourselves on our high performance. But no unit is perfect, and for one reason or another, we were at about 95 percent completion with the required training for that year. Mind you, we were still far better than any other organization and still had several months to complete the tasks. But it did not matter, Chad expected full green. But screw that guy. I was not going to lie for him, so I wrote up an accurate accounting of where we stood. A bright yellow box of truth gleamed in the middle of the slide like a shining "eff you" to Chad. For a few moments I just stared at the email I had drafted with the attached report.

Should I send it?

I could feel my pulse quicken, hear the thumping of my heart pounding in my ears. With a swift jab, I smashed down on the send button. Almost immediately, I got called to his office. I steeled myself for the expected confrontation, marched to his office, and reported. He glared up at me from his desk, still smiling, but it didn't reach his eyes.

"Great to see you. Please close the door and have a seat," he welcomed as he gestured to the chair across from him, the thin veneer of civility and calm cracking ever so slightly.

"I couldn't help but notice the report you submitted. Has there been some sort of mistake?"

This was a part of the charade. He knew it wasn't a mistake. Of course, he knew. And I knew exactly what he wanted me to do. And *he* knew that I knew what he wanted me to do, but he could not come straight out and say it. That would have been over the line. So instead, we did this stupid dance. He would gush about how important this briefing was, and how we should highlight all the hard work of the men. Then I would explain that—while I was indeed proud of the team—it was physically impossible for us to have completed the task in the time available. And around and around we went, back and forth for almost an hour, neither of us giving an inch. His false air of professionalism and calm had begun to wane and, possibly for the first time, I was beginning to see his true emotions piercing through.

"So, are you saying that you have not adequately prepared your men?" he jabbed, as his face grew to an even darker shade of red. He stood from his chair, "because I want leaders who can get the job done. Not 95, not 99, but 100 percent! Got me?"

The threat was not lost on me. Unconsciously, my hand drifted up to my chest, feeling the small oval medallion hanging around my neck beneath my uniform. I couldn't see it but knew without looking the familiar image of a man on horseback slaying a dragon. Even through the fabric of my tan t-shirt, I could almost feel the raised letters spelling "Saint George, Pray for Us." A brief smile darted across my lips as a happy memory shot through my mind of my wife gifting me the necklace when I joined the Catholic church.

During their confirmation, every Catholic selects one of the canonized saints with whom they feel a connection. There's a big misconception about saints from non-Catholics, my former self included. Having converted later in life, I'm very familiar with seeing things from both sides of the theological aisle. Many people think that Catholics view saints as mystical, magical people who achieved god-status while on earth. But that's not necessarily true. Technically, everyone who has made it to heaven is considered a saint in the eyes of the church. Your grandma, your great-uncle, that nice old lady who used to live down the street. Everyone who made it to heaven is a saint. The only difference for a canonized saint is that, based on a variety of tests, the Catholic Church believes they have proof that the person is in heaven. And, because they're in heaven, they can intercede on our behalf and talk to God for us.

Saint George always stood out to me. He's a familiar name amongst adolescent Catholic boys due to his renown for slaying a dragon. When compared to all the pious, peace-loving martyrs, this epic dragon slaying, elite Roman soldier seems pretty captivating to a kid in Sunday school. And as awesome as all that is, it's not why I picked him. The thing that called to me about Saint George was his unrelenting, courageous commitment to the truth. Time and time again, despite his high rank and status within the Roman army, he unashamedly stood up for what he knew was right. When faced with punishment, exile, and even death, he remained steadfast at his post, upholding both his obligation to the military and to his faith. So, in that moment, as I could feel the small medallion beneath my shirt, I was once again reminded of the courage of Saint George and prayed for the strength to follow his example.

Chad grew louder and louder, now at the point of yelling. I could see the cracks in his veneer of civility growing and spreading, revealing the seething anger within. I rose to meet Chad's gaze, stone-faced and said as calmly and as forcefully as I could.

"I'm not going to lie for you, sir."

He fell quiet as he glared back. An eternity passed as we stared each other down, neither backing away from the electricity pulsing between us.

Finally, Chad broke down.

"Fuck!" he cried out as the mask of politeness shattered completely, and all pretenses fell away. He had spent so much time and effort crafting this whole persona. *Funny*, I thought, *how easily it all came tumbling down. One small nudge and the whole house of cards came crashing down.* Then, another realization took hold—how had he survived this long, all show and no substance? I guess no one had ever called him out before. Maybe he thought if he kept selling his snake-oil hard enough, he'd never have to face reality. But that ended that day.

Exasperated, he flopped back down into his chair, defeated. For the first time I could see the man he really was. Not the fake façade of the boss, but the man himself. He seemed so sad and pitiful. I almost felt sorry for him. In a way, Chad was a genius—a savant of self-propaganda. If other, truly good commanders had even a tenth of Chad's publicizing abilities they would skyrocket through the ranks. But unfortunately, Chad had no weight to back up his outlandish claims of excellence. He was so afraid of letting anyone see his inadequacies that he had constructed this entire persona to hide behind. But with his patina of perfection now marred by that tiny yellow box, Chad seemed to lose his edge. A god who bleeds is no longer a god.

Despite being a horrific boss, I gleaned two sacred golden nuggets of wisdom from my experience with Chad. The first of these was that, for better or for worse, perception matters. As frustrating as it might be, leadership doesn't always have the clearest understanding of what their subordinates are doing. Think of it—how often does your boss actually see you at work? Not often. They're super busy and probably only make it out to your training a handful of times. And even then, it is only for a few minutes. You could be out there saving the world, but your boss doesn't have a crystal ball and unless you are showing them the great work you're doing, they aren't going to have any way of knowing. And the way we show these things happens through very deliberate mechanisms.

Storyboards, trackers, reports—these are the language of progress. Lots of people are out there doing great things, but if you never show your work, it doesn't count. Yeah, of course it matters in the "doing good for goodness' sake" sense of things, but you aren't going to get recognition. Now, a lot of people feel uncomfortable with this idea; they don't want to be a showoff. Humility is certainly a virtue, and you don't want to be one of those pompous pricks like Chad. But it's not about you; it is about getting recognition for your team. Under your leadership, those men and women have worked to the bone, and they deserve to be acknowledged by someone higher up than you. Now it is your job to tell that story. With pictures and crystal-clear language, spell out what an amazing job your people are doing and then smack your boss over the head every single day with it. Not for you, but for your people. Be an advocate for their sake. If you don't, just know that much of their hard work is going to get overlooked because guys like Chad aren't going to let the opportunity slip by.

The second crucial lesson was to never sacrifice your honor. I remember talking about honor and integrity a lot as a cadet. In almost every class or professional development session we'd have some deep philosophical message about the importance of living up to the Army values. At the time, I envisioned myself engaging in intense moral battles with life and death consequences. But they never really came. Everything seemed so benign and not *that* big of a deal. Yellow or green, does it even matter that much? Certainly, it's not worth falling on my sword, right? But it is within these small moments that you truly decide who you are. Seemingly trivial, our split-second decisions have cascading effects that can lead us down tremendously different paths. When you hear about leaders making outrageously poor ethical choices, you can almost always trace back through a chain of lesser offenses. But these seemingly inconsequential transgressions grow over time into ever more severe missteps. Frankly, had I had the courage to stand up to Chad's foolishness earlier, we probably wouldn't have had such a severe clash.

I'll be honest, there will be negative consequences for holding firm for righteousness. People will like you less. You might even get a lesser evaluation. Of course, you shouldn't be a jerk about it and should always remain respectful and humble. But even still, you'll face a backlash.

"Why are you making this hard for everyone?"

"Why are you being such a tool?"

You will be shocked at the social pressure that mounts when you stand firm. But trust me when I tell you, the reward always far outweighs the negative. Sometimes, it can take quite a while; however, in the long run, staying true to yourself always pays off.

Chad sat slumped in his chair, face down on the desk. He looked totally defeated. With an exhausted wave of his hand, Chad beckoned me to leave as he gestured to the door. As I walked out of his office, I could hear him pleading from behind me.

"Just ... just make it green."

Funny, I thought. *That was the first time he hadn't thanked me.*

For many of us, the idea of working with perception is an uncomfortable, almost detestable idea. We like clear-cut, black and white answers. Two plus two is four—always. You either did the thing or you didn't do the thing, there's no middle ground. Like Yoda said, "there is no try, only do." The idea of perception is too wishy-washy, too in the gray areas; it feels like you are manipulating or lying. We like facts. There's not *your* truth or *my* truth; there is just *the* truth. I couldn't agree more with this sentiment. But, as I've come to appreciate, the truth is often far more complicated than a first-order approximation. As a leader, it's often crucial that you parse through these higher-order complexities and get acquainted with the subtleties of an issue. For example, it's simply a fact that, whether you like it or not, there is a subjective component to assessing the quality and performance of an organization. I suggest learning to navigate this complex network for the betterment of your team.

Not everything fits neatly into a box, and it is up to you to influence those decisions for the better. Even something as simple as recognizing the difference between good and evil can be a challenge if you aren't paying attention.

13 ···· JUMPMASTER!

"Those who look for the bad in people will surely find it." –
Abraham Lincoln

I have always thought of myself as a kind and open-hearted person. Since childhood, I attended Sunday school every week, prayed for the poor, and volunteered regularly. I even smiled and greeted people on the street. Of course, I heard about things like prejudice and hatred in the news or in history books, but that was about bad people—certainly not me. I was a good person and thus incapable of such evil.

I was wrong.

In my mid-twenties, as you recall, I deployed to Afghanistan with my Combat Engineer Company. Our primary mission was something called "route clearance." This meant that we would drive ahead of a different unit looking for Improvised Explosive Devises (IEDs) to clear their way. It takes a bit of time to get rid of the explosives once you find them, so the enemy would often try to attack while we were dealing with the IED they had set out.

Several months into the deployment, one of our units got into another TIC (Troops in Contact) while on a mission. While they were interrogating a suspected IED, which the enemy had shoved inside a dead goat and left alongside the road, our guys started to receive small-arms fire from a nearby rock pile. The group of four insurgents, probably the same ones that emplaced the goat bomb, had been waiting for American troops to run into their little surprise. Undiscouraged that their ruse had been unsuccessful, they switched tactics and decided to shoot at us instead. In response, our guys immediately began laying down covering fire as they maneuvered upon the enemy threat.

As the Company XO, I was several miles away in our TOC (Tactical Operations Center). My staff and I worked with the Battalion Battle Captain to receive reports, ensure additional assets were available, and track the battle. Thanks to our high-speed capabilities, we were even able to watch the firefight from our "eyes in the sky" and provide real-time feedback to the troops on the ground. For my entire young adult life, ever since I watched terrorists crash into the twin towers, all I had ever wanted to do was join the Army, deploy, and bring the fight to them.

But there I was, spending most of my deployed time behind a desk as the XO. It was frustrating, especially watching my friends leave the wire everyday while I was stuck, sheltered safely on base. Sure, I managed to hop on a few patrols, but those opportunities were sparse. Most of the time I was relegated to the TOC. But despite the daily shame of watching my friends go into combat while I stayed and sat in the air conditioning, I became determined to be the best damned observer that ever lived. If we could help them even a little, it was like I was still participating. And so, we glued our eyes to the screen, calling up anything we thought could help.

Everything was going well. By this point, our men were no strangers to combat and were operating as they had a hundred times before. They had already maneuvered into position and fired on the bad dudes from two sides. The insurgents jumped up every once in a while to blindly spray bullets towards us, but our team was focused and disciplined, working as two parts of the same whole. Like a deadly game of chess viewed from a thousand feet above, we watched as our troops maneuvered for the crushing blow. You could clearly see the right flank squeezing in as the front flank started to lift and shift fire—a picture perfect battle drill. It was just a matter of time before the enemy would either run away or our men would destroy them. I was rooting for the latter.

Then, weirdly, an old man walked out from a small patch of trees jutting away from rocky ground about fifty meters away. He stumbled forward into the light and started meandering towards the open area where the fighting was taking place.

Where had he come from?

The closest town was still a few miles down the road.

How had we missed this guy?

Had we gotten so sucked into the excitement of the battle that we forgot to keep an eye for civilians?

We scanned the area for nearby houses or cars, rapidly trying to figure out how he got there, but there was nothing—just rocks, dust, and scorched earth with a few lonesome trees dotting the terrain. The barren landscape merged with the ominous, looming mountains in the distance. I decided to divert one of our cameras to zoom in and get a better look at the guy, hoping to better understand the mystery of the old man. He was rather unremarkable and seemed pretty much like the rest of the other old men in the villages. He had the normal skinny frame with the addition of an old man belly. His beard was long and white but recently manicured. The traditional long garment he wore, which we typically referred to as a "man-dress," was tattered but relatively clean. His good hygiene was a bit odd, pretty much everyone we saw was covered in dust and sweat, but he'd probably had his monthly bath recently. The old dude wasn't anything special.

Still, as commonplace as he was, his awkward behavior made me uncomfortable. I couldn't put my finger on it; he wasn't threatening or aggressive. The poor old man seemed lost as he aimlessly wandered around in a daze. I shook off the odd sensation clawing at the back of my mind and focused on monitoring the radio traffic again. It was nothing, just some old guy who got lost or something. Perhaps he was in shock at the sudden outburst of violence. I know I'd be pretty shaken up if, while on my morning stroll, dudes started popping off shots in my direction. Then again, by this point in the war such small arms skirmishes were relatively commonplace. In fact, the bloody violence that would make national news in the states seemed like a daily part of life over there, even long before the war had begun.

Another idea struck me; the old dude was probably high. Though grown further to our southeast, Afghanistan was well known for its poppy fields. In a land seemingly filled with only dust and death, the blissful respite of opium pervaded every corner of the country. Or, for all we knew, he was a nice old man with dementia; someone's grandpa who had wondered too far from home. It was not as if they had great assisted living facilities to care for the elderly. But whatever the case, if we did not act fast this old dude was about to get shot, so we had to act quickly.

A few of our men shouted the plan over the radio and then rushed over to protect the old man. From the safety of the TOC, I watched as they surrounded the man to cover him from the gunfire and then shepherd him back to safety. He might have been a crazy old coot, but at least he was going to be okay. When day after day you feel like you're fighting the same battles, it's easy to get discouraged and wonder if you're making a difference. But this was a clear win. No doubt about it, we'd saved this old man's life. Through the intense zoom of our imaging, I thought I could even see a look of calm and relief rush over the old man's weathered face. Over the radio, they confirmed.

"We did it. We got him. Everything's good."

Then our screen flashed white before it went dark. A plume of smoke now erupted from where my men had been standing. In the TOC, we stared at the screen, befuddled by the weird and unexpected patch of scorched earth, almost forming the shape of a bizarre flower. A few instants later, we heard a distant rumble, like thunder rolling through the valley.

What just happened?

Did the video freeze?

Why had everyone stopped moving?

It took me a second to understand. I could not figure out why everyone was lying on the ground. For the briefest of moments, it reminded me of one of those old-time synchronized swimming routines where the pretty lady jumps up from the middle of a starburst. But there was no pretty lady in the middle. In her place was the charred black crater where the old man had stood. Then it hit me. Like a bolt of lightning, I was struck by ten thousand volts of realization that shook me to my core. This motherfucker had blown himself up. He knew we would come to rescue him. That was the plan. The insurgents who had started the attack were just a diversion. This old man was the real attack all along. The fresh haircut, the clean clothes, the sense of calm—it all made sense. He was planning to meet Allah.

They knew we would try to protect the old man and bring him back to safety. And knowing this, this worthless piece of human garbage—this *demon*—had exploited our kindness and our mercy, sneaking in like the Trojan Horse. Such pure evil was, at the time, unfathomable to me. But, it should not have been.

Savages, every one of them, I thought.

There was no honor or justice in their depraved, backwards society. In fact, such barbarism was so common amongst these animals, that we even had a name for the damned tactic. An "s-vest" (suicide vest) we called it. It was something I heard about in training. but had never witnessed its horror before that moment. The rest of the men made short work of the remaining enemy, utterly wiping them from existence in a matter of minutes. Still, the white-hot anger burned. I wished I could have been there to pull the trigger. Then, I wished we could have brought the insurgents back to life, just so we could kill them all again. But there I sat, cool and comfortable in that fucking air-conditioned TOC.

Thanks to the heroic actions of our medic, who in the midst of the fighting sprinted through a hail of gunfire to treat the wounded, some of our soldiers survived. In the blink of an eye, our medic assessed which people he had a chance of saving, and then got to work resuscitating those he could. Three of our men are alive today because Doc pulled them out of death's doorway. Maybe that gave a few of our people closure. Maybe they slept better knowing that we killed more of them than they did of us, but I doubt it. For me, at least, there was no closure, only hate and rage.

The injured were swiftly medevaced and received life-saving care. The bodies of our dead were recovered and a ceremony was held in their honor. Everyone was encouraged to see the chaplain if they needed to talk. A few did, but not many. I certainly did not feel like I had a right to be affected. After all, I wasn't even really there; I had just watched it on a screen. If anyone needed help, it was my men who were *in* the fight—not me. Instead, we all just buried the pain and moved out, determined to somehow pay back this injustice tenfold. As weeks went by, everything seemed to get back to normal. But this was a façade. I still smiled and engaged with the locals, but I no longer trusted them; all I saw were potential threats.

Savages, I thought again. *Every one of them.*

I still joked with my friends despite my growing anger. At church services, we would talk about "loving thy neighbor" and I would say the words, but they were empty. Eventually, to my shame, I stopped going to services and praying altogether. Steadily, I started to shut out the light and love of God, which had been such an important presence in my life. In its void burned only hatred and a growing darkness.

A few months later, as mentioned earlier, I was injured during a mortar attack. I do not remember anything about the event. In fact, an entire week prior to the attack was completely wiped from my memory. However, I have been informed that a mortar round exploded near our TOC. Once everyone recovered from the blast, they found me passed out in my office. I was transported to the medic station, flown to a larger care facility, and eventually loaded on a plane for Germany to receive prolonged care. But like I said, I don't remember any of this.

My one and only period of consciousness was during the flight to Germany—although, to be perfectly honest, it might also be a dream or a hallucination. I had been heavily medicated and cannot really be sure. But then again, it doesn't matter. Real or imaginary, the events aboard that flight have had a lasting and immeasurable impact on my life.

I opened my eyes and found myself aboard an aircraft. My arms, legs, and even head were strapped down to a board. I had no idea of how I got there, where we were going, or any idea of what was going on. All I could figure out was that this was the inside of a C-17. As a paratrooper, I was no stranger to the C-130 or the C-17 aircrafts, as they are the primary troop carriers for airborne operations. I had spent countless hours crammed inside one of them, preparing to jump out. And because of this experience, combined with a mixture of head trauma and medication, I erroneously concluded that I was about to be thrown from the plane. Only one problem: I did not have a parachute.

Immediately, I began screaming for the Jumpmaster. It is standard procedure to notify the Jumpmaster if you have any issues with your parachute. Of course, not having a parachute all together certainly qualifies as a problem.

"Jumpmaster! Jumpmaster!" I screamed over and over again, hoping someone would hear my cry. At any moment the door would open, and I would be hurled out into the abyss. I tried to move and wave my arms to get someone's attention, but it was hopeless. My whole body ached as I wrenched against my restraints, but I could not budge.

"Jumpmaster!" I feebly sobbed as tears began to roll down my cheeks.

Then, a man appeared out of my periphery. Fading in and out of consciousness, I watched him timidly approach. His face was dark and weathered. His long wispy beard draped over his now dirty robes. Like a slap in the face, a thought struck me, and adrenaline coursed through my veins as I recognized him. It was the old man; the one we had saved.

No, it couldn't be.

He was dead; this must be a different man.

Or was he?

My head hurt and everything was fuzzy; I couldn't tell what was real. Images raced through my mind as a new nightmare emerged. Our soldiers rushing to save the man. The sudden puff of smoke and the bodies stretched out in the sand. I saw all of them, burnt and bloodied—my friends, my brothers. Renewed by a sudden overwhelming flood of both hatred and fear, again I cried out.

"Jumpmaster! Jumpmaster!"

This time I wasn't scared about being thrown from the plane. All I wanted was for someone to release my restraints so that I could beat the life from this piece of garbage. I envisioned myself, hands around his neck, bashing his head into the ground again and again, watching the light fade from his eyes. But it had to be soon, it had to be now. Either I escaped my restraints to kill him, or he was absolutely going to kill me. I yelled for the Jumpmaster one last time before I began screaming at the man.

"I'll kill you! I'll kill you!" I shouted as spit sprayed like venom from my mouth.

I kept on like that for a long time, screaming at the man, then for the Jumpmaster to release me, then back at the man. On and on until my throat was dry and there was no air left in my lungs. But no one heard, no one came. It was just me and the old man.

Eventually, I could shout no more and fell silent, resigned and awaiting the inevitable blast to come. But there was no explosion, no attack. Instead, amidst the constant whine of the plane's engines, a soft and tender melody arose from my would-be assailant. It was like nothing that I had ever heard before. In his deep and thickly accented voice, the man sang out in his native tongue. I could not understand the words, but it was sweet and kind and unmistakably a lullaby. With his cracked and wrinkled hands, the man reached out and brushed away my tears. He stroked my hair and smiled down at me, the whole while singing his song.

It was beautiful.

I imagined him at the foot of his grandchildren's beds, singing them to sleep just as my own mother sang to me when I was young. I did not know the language, but I understood his meaning.

"You are safe. You are loved."

A wave of emotions washed over me, laying bare the error of my sinful heart. How easily I had let hatred and prejudice fill my soul. There is no question, had I been able to move, I would have killed him. With every fiber of my being, I hated him. To even look at him filled me with rage and disgust. And yet, when he saw me, broken and weak, spewing such vitriol in his direction, he responded with only love and compassion. Through his eyes, I could see myself, possessed by the same demons I had sworn to fight, and it shamed me. And so, I wept.

As I wept, I felt as if the black tar that had grafted to my soul was being excised from my body. It was like a scab, putrid and festering, had been ripped from my flesh to reveal healthy, new skin beneath. Though it hurt, it was a joyous pain, a pain of rebirth and renewal. This whole time, the man continued to sing and wipe away my tears. He'd smile and pat my head. Slowly, my breathing began to steady and my pain subsided. And after a minute, or an eternity, I finally felt at peace. I closed my eyes and drifted off to sleep, comforted by the melody of a song I did not know.

Let me be very clear, there are terrible people on this earth. Sadly, some have strayed so far that, by their continued choices, they have allowed themselves to become the incarnation of evil. The depth of their sadistic depravity is unfathomable; they are an abomination. If they get ahold of you, there will be no mercy or temperance. They do not listen to reason or show restraint. If given the chance, they will end you and everything you hold dear without the slightest hesitation. It is not only right and just, but imperative that you remain vigilant in defending yourself and those in your charge from their evil grasp.

But as you build these walls of defense, be careful not to stack them so high that you close yourself off from the light and imprison yourself in darkness. As surely as there is evil, there is also good. Blinding yourself of either will result in your downfall. But by recognizing evil while arming ourselves with righteousness, we prepare for the ongoing battle. Some people need killing, but not everyone.

In the immortal words of the great Dr. Martin Luther King Jr., "Darkness cannot drive out darkness; only light can do that. Hate cannot drive out hate; only love can do that." Look, we are not Doctors Without Borders; this is the Profession of Arms. When it comes down to it, your whole job is either killing bad guys, or helping someone else kill bad guys. It isn't glorious or funny or cool. It's a terrible thing we endure so that the rest of the population can know peace and freedom. We battle in the twilight, between the light and the dark, in the hopes that no one else will ever know the terror that lurks just beyond the shadows. But as you battle on that edge, take care not to go too far and let yourself become consumed.

When I finally awoke, I was in a hospital bed and the man was nowhere to be found. Days had passed since my time on the plane. I talked to several people—nurses, doctors, even other patients, but no one seemed to have any knowledge of the man. It was like he disappeared, or maybe he had never really been there at all. Since then, I have spent many nights thinking of the old man on the plane. Was he a drug-fueled hallucination? A manifestation of all the internal struggle which had been playing out in my mind? Or maybe he was an angel? As crazy as it sounds, I've thought that God might have sent down a messenger to teach me a lesson and bring me back into His light. Or, could it be possible that he was just a kind old man who saw a stranger in need and reached out to sooth an aching heart? I honestly don't know. Perhaps he was all three.

Learning to recognize the good and the bad in others amidst the chaos of a broken world can be challenging. But even more challenging can be to recognize those things within ourselves. So often, we focus our attention outward, myopically focused on those around us. When we do finally turn our sights inward, it is tempting to conform to what we see nearby. But recall, you have been designed for something special. Find that goodness and let it shine through for the betterment of the world.

14 ···· SILLY SOCKS

I'm not a big, fat panda. I'm the big, fat panda! – Poe, *Kung Fu Panda*

As I walked the long, uphill path towards the battalion headquarters, I looked down for possibly the thousandth time, unconsciously checking my bootlaces. I don't know why, but a constant fear loomed in the back of my mind that, at any moment, one of my laces might mistakenly come out and a gung-ho sergeant major would jump out from the bushes to yell at me for not being squared away. Then, like the loose thread on a sweater, the tug on an errant boot lace would lead to my unraveling and nakedness of how un-squared away I truly was. So, like one of those germaphobes who spends all their time washing their hands, afraid to get sick, I found myself continuously tucking my laces further into my boots to ensure I was never caught off guard.

That's when I saw it, a small patch of swirly blue and yellow cotton poking up from around my ankle. Immediately, I dropped to the ground as swiftly as if shots were being fired and covered it.

Had anyone seen?

How long had it been sticking out?

How could I be so stupid?

I forcefully shoved the colorful fabric deeper into my boot, safely hidden beneath the thick green nylon of the Army-approved socks. Slowly, I slyly scanned the area, cautiously shifting my gaze left and right to see if anyone had been watching. But no one had seemed to notice—just a bunch of identical camouflaged figures hustling about their day, off to fight the next crisis of the moment. A sigh of relief escaped my lips, and for a brief moment, I allowed myself to smile at the thought of my mischievous little secret. I wore silly socks while in uniform.

Such a strange and foolish compulsion, I'd picked up the habit years prior as a cadet. At first, it started as a joke, a goof shared between myself and the universe. I've always considered myself to be a joyful person— like a mushroom, I'm a fun guy—so when I first saw the pair of zany socks hanging on the rack, I thought it would be a silly gag to wear them under my uniform. But after the first day wearing them, something deeper immerged. It wasn't just a joke, but a symbol. It was a totem of my true self, surrounded by an exterior of stalwart professionalism, hidden from a scrutinizing world. Whenever I felt trapped or out of place, I could wiggle my toes and feel the secret fabric, reminding me of the guy I was inside. Eventually, the humor left altogether, and the habit was more of a silent rebellion, not just of the strict regimented profession I had chosen, but against the expectations and pressure I had put on myself.

As a child, I had one of those stretchy goo-filled balls. I enjoyed the squishy feel as I squeezed the ball in my palm. But no matter how I clenched my fist, no matter how tightly I tried to push the object into the tight shape I wanted, a small bit would always shoot out, seeping through the gaps in my fingers. That was what the socks had come to mean to me. They were a manifestation of the neglected inner-me sneaking between the cracks as I tried to force myself into the mold of someone else. And over time, as I became unable to force myself into the person I thought I was supposed to be, I grew angry. Somehow, I never seemed able to conquer and kill that part of me that refused to die.

What's the old adage?

No matter where you go, you're always there.

It's not like I was spending every night shaking my fist at the sky and shouting to the heavens, but a part of me was always angry. I was mad at myself for not being the person I thought I was supposed to be. My inner voice screamed, "Just get it together! Don't mess this up!" I was mad at the Army for being something I so desperately wanted but felt like I never fit into—a square peg in a round hole. I was mad at all my friends and colleagues who seemed to get it. Where I always felt out of place, they seemed to fit into their roles so easily. Perfect little soldiers, small and fast, executing their tasks with a seriousness I could never seem to muster.

Each year we'd go to the photography center to get our professional photos updated. These were the images that would pop up anytime someone would search for your profile on a myriad of Army systems, so it was important to always look your best. Standing in line in our fancy "Class A" uniforms, we'd take turns checking each other to make sure our medals were positioned in just the right place. Guys even brought pocket rulers as a spot-check to make sure nothing was off by a sixteenth of an inch. Others passed around lint rollers to catch that one stray hair that landed on their jackets. Then, the image of professional perfection, they'd march into the booth, stand stiffly at attention, and stare deadeye and scowling into the camera. And each year, as I watched my friends go, I would think to myself, "This is the year. This is the year I don't smile." But every year, I'd get to my mark and prepare my grumpiest face and just as they would be about to take the picture, I wouldn't be able to help myself and flash a giant, toothy grin. Life's just too awesome not to smile.

It was infuriating.

What made it worse was that I genuinely wanted to be that perfect image I had floating around my mind of the classic iron warrior. I wanted to be every bit the steely-eyed, serious man-of-war I saw reflected in so many of my friends and colleagues. Don't get me wrong, I've always been serious about doing a good job and getting the mission accomplished. I just never understood why we couldn't also have fun. Since when was "boring" a prerequisite for success? Nevertheless, I was self-aware enough to recognize when I was straying too far from the norm. I just needed to focus, needed to buckle down more. If only I could come in a bit earlier and stay later, if I could do that extra report or be more detailed in my planning, if I could read just one more of the painfully boring military books, then I might be able to become the super-officer I thought I was supposed to be.

But none of it helped.

Yeah, of course I learned and developed as a leader, I became more capable of recognizing and squashing my quirkiness, but fundamentally, deep down, I was still the same silly dude I'd always been. No matter what I did or where I went, I was always there. Maybe this wasn't for me.

Honestly, being in the military was the only thing I'd ever wanted. Growing up, seeing my dad in uniform, I never imagined myself doing anything except serving. But, alas, as much as I was the son of a warrior, devoted and hardworking and tenacious, I was also my mother's son. For every football practice my dad took me to, my mother enrolled me into a theater class or music competition. As comfortable as I felt navigating through the woods or fighting on the gridiron, I also enjoyed singing and dancing and telling jokes. I don't know, maybe that weird combination was too much of a contradiction.

Obviously, I wasn't fitting in.

For goodness sakes, I couldn't even wear the dang uniform without sneaking my stupid silly socks on underneath. Maybe it just wasn't for me. For quite a while, I sat with this realization. It didn't matter what I did, I was never going to be that super squared away erudite who spends his waking hours devouring historic military readings and developing training calendars, and then runs marathons in his sleep. It's never going to happen, so why even try. I was so tired of banging my head into the wall, trying to be something I wasn't. With startling swiftness, I became despondent, wallowing in self-pity as a million tiny violins in my mind sang a song entitled, "Woe Is Me." But suddenly, amidst the symphony of self-pity, a thought struck me. A realization every bit as timeless and profound as anything from Plato or Aristotle hit me right in the face.

Who freaking cares?

Seriously, where had I originally gotten this image in my mind of what "right" looked like? And even if there was an ideal Army officer, was there actually anyone standing by, measuring me against this make-believe standard? And even if there was, why should I care? I asked myself, if you worked your butt off and become the absolutely best you can be, but never become "good enough" in the eyes of these imaginary gate keepers, could you live with that?

The answer—heck yeah, I could.

Now, don't get it twisted, I am *not* saying that we shouldn't try to better ourselves. There are a lot of voices, especially in today's day and age, telling folks, "You're perfect just the way you are. All the problems in your life, those are the world's fault, not yours." Sorry to break it to you, but none of us—not even you—are perfect. Of course, there are things we need to work on as we grow and improve, but the key is that we've got to follow our own paths.

There's a fabulous movie called *Kung Fu Panda*, which I absolutely love. Besides being one of the few genuinely entertaining family movies that can be enjoyed by kids and adults alike, it has an incredible message which continues to resonate. In the movie, the old and stern kung fu master, Shifu, is frustrated in his efforts to train his newly assigned student, the goofy, uncoordinated, flabby panda named Poe. At every turn, Poe fails miserably in even the most basic of training. But then, after witnessing the famished Poe miraculously climb to the top of the cupboard and devour his friend's secret stash of delicious almond cookies while performing a perfect split, Shifu uncovers a radically new way to approach training, unlocking untapped potential and transforming Poe's oddities into strengths. Later, when faced with a similar problem of how to train a group of other flabby, uncoordinated pandas, the now Master Poe, exclaims, "I don't have to turn you into me. I have to turn you into *you*!"

We hear a lot about diversity nowadays, but I think many of these conversations miss the point—devolving it into a derivative, shallow view of the idea. As such, the word often develops a negative connotation due to a pervasive and myopic obsession with immutable physical characteristics. Consider for a moment a bag of trail mix and a bag of Skittles. One is a complex, harmonious conglomeration of flavors as various parts, delicious in their own right, but tremendously different in shape and size and color that comes together to make a symphony of flavor. The other is a bag of sugar pills of varying hues. Certainly, our physical qualities can impact how we engage with and thus view the world, but a failure to grasp a broader approach neglects a deeper, richer understanding of the totality of individuals. Real diversity cultivates our peculiarities in a synergistic approach as we pursue better mission accomplishment. Such diversity is vital to an organization and something you can take an active role in contributing towards.

Don't hide yourself. Don't blindly conform to the cookie-cutter image you might have of the ideal warrior. Yes, of course, some areas you should conform. Be competent and be good at PT. Present yourself professionally. Become educated in military art and science. Live honorably. Oh, and for goodness sakes, get a dang haircut! But don't lose yourself. Not all, but many of those weird little things that make you, *you,* are also the things that you can leverage to better the organization. Those are the things that no one else is providing and it is your job to add those things to the mix. God made you unique. Yes, we are all formed in His image, but we are all in his unique image. Like peering through a keyhole and only seeing part of a portrait, through our lives we share an exclusive glimpse of God's infinite majesty with the world. Don't hide that light.

After discovering this part of myself, after becoming comfortable with who I was and who I was supposed to be, I was able to reflect on my journey of discovery. Looking back, I realized four important points—more golden nuggets for the ole treasure box. First and foremost, I became way better at my job and, subsequently, much happier when I stopped pretending to be a different person. All that energy I had expended on acting out this imaginary role, I could now use to dive, headfirst into projects using my unique set of gifts. I started going "full Logan," as one great boss would later tell me.

Secondly, I understood that the only real gatekeeper was myself. For the most part, no one was judging me for being too quirky or different. There was no chorus of people laughing at my every move, pointing out how I struggled to fit in. Sure, leaders would point out areas for improvement, which is a valuable part of their job, but they did that with everyone. Looking back, I see that almost all the restrictions and false expectations I placed on myself were a direct reflection of my own insecurities from failing to live up to an imaginary standard of perfection I concocted. The only person holding me back was myself.

Of course, there were haters. There are always "haters." But let's be honest, they were never going to like me anyway. Even if I could have become more in line with their own image of the perfect soldier, they probably found something else about me not to like. The shade they threw said much more about their own insecurities than my failings. But those people, those true haters, are much less common than you might think. The little voice in your head says that they are everywhere, secretly watching and judging your every move. However, that's just not true. No one cares about your differences as long as you perform. For the most part, I discovered that others like confident, self-assured people who they can count on to get the job done. All the other stuff that seemed like a big deal, really wasn't.

The third thing I realized, was about the nature of my progression. I never fit those pieces together until I began to retell the story of my evolution through self-acceptance, but as I wrote down the words, something about it felt familiar. First, the rejection of my true self, denying the parts of me that didn't fit and hiding them away, just like the silly socks I buried under my uniform. Then I grew angry with my inability to keep that part hidden away and with the organization that, at the time I thought, set an impossible standard. Later, not yet willing to give in, I pleaded with myself, begging me to work just a bit harder to change. But unsuccessful in changing my identity, I grew despondent and depressed. Finally, miraculously, I managed to pull myself out of the miasma and learn my worth by accepting the person God made me to be. Denial, anger, bargaining, depression, acceptance—like a flash, it struck me—these are the stages of grief. But grieving *what*? I asked myself.

Grieving the loss of the "pretend self" I had created in my mind. A collection of movie heroes, influential military leaders, and iconic professionals, I had forged this idol of the perfect me. But that was a fantasy, no more realistic than wanting to grow up to be a tyrannosaurus. For a long time, I'd kept that image, like a child clinging to a blankie, comforted by its familiarity. But fantasies are for children, and I had to let it go. It was hard and painful. It required loss. But only by letting go of this cartoon image was I finally able to see the fuller, more magnificently complex image of my best self. It is a future, better version that is still truly me.

Lastly, after all the struggle and growth, I realized that I don't wear the socks anymore. Sure, I might slip them on during my off-time, but I certainly never wear them in uniform. I don't need them anymore. The part of me they represented is no longer hidden, but a vibrant and integral part of who I am as a leader.

With a deeper appreciation for the subtleties of leadership, your potential for success is limitless. Please, I encourage you to eagerly take these golden nuggets. But don't stop there; continue to search for your own riches, constantly adding to your wealth of professional knowledge. Like an old frontiersman mining the earth, scour the landscape of your own experiences and pluck out new wisdom. I promise, such moments are littered throughout your adventures. You only need to be ready to stop and pick them up.

.... PART FOUR: RESPECT YOUR JOURNEY

15 ···· DID HE MAKE IT?

Talk low, talk slow, and don't say too much. – John Wayne

It might not seem like it now, but I promise, time is *flying* by. You're going to blink your eyes and five years will have passed. This is especially true now that you have joined an excellent team to fulfill your purpose, risen above your old trauma, and are now absolutely crushing it at your job. During the excitement and chaos of life, it's easy to become drawn into the crisis of the moment. We're always churning so hard to solve the next problem, like an endless game of whack-a-mole, that we forget to stop and reflect. Such nonstop action is certainly engaging and, frankly, is a part of the fun of a high-paced job. But there is a lot more going on that you don't want to miss. Stop and take a moment to respect your story. Learn from what is going on and see the bigger picture.

For me, my journey into the military began with my grandfather. Grandpa had flat feet. He was also kind of a grumpy, mean old fart who constantly smoked a pipe and grumbled about all that was going wrong around him. He and Grandma lived on an Oklahoma farm along a lake in a small house he'd built with his own two hands. He was old-fashioned, both in temperament and in drink choice. The carpet in his living room had a path worn out connecting his colossal recliner where he'd watch his westerns to the built-in bar which he'd constructed from scratch. He was a large sturdy man at 6'2" who slicked his dark black hair back with pomade and smelled of sweet tobacco and bourbon. He was loyal, hardworking, persnickety, stubborn, and commanding. But curiously, the feature which would have the most defining impact on the course of his life was this obscure podiatric ailment.

Unquestionably, Grandpa possessed an incredible work ethic. Even in his later years, the man would spend every moment of daylight working on his farm. He would wake up before the sunrise and then disappear into the fields, only to reemerge for dinner, covered in dirt and sweat from a day's hard labor. I'm not tremendously sure that he ever even sold his crops, at least not a significant amount. He grew everything from apples and lemons to lettuce; he even dabbled in beekeeping—but none of it was on a major scale. No, it wasn't about making money. We never spoke about it, but I think he just enjoyed the work. Years of toiling under the sun had left him rugged and hard as steel. And though good for weathering the harshness of life, this rough exterior did not make for a very comforting companion to a young boy.

Most of my childhood memories of Grandpa centered on my constant shortcomings. The rest of the family would joke that the only thing higher than his expectation was his blood pressure. Ironically, he mandated that—at all times—we referred to him as "Sweet Grandpa Bob." Now, there are many adjectives that could be used to describe him, but "sweet" is not among them. Nevertheless, failing to address him by this honorific would inevitably result in you getting a swat on the butt, followed by a lengthy tale about the state of today's youth and their flagrant lack of respect for their elders. In all fairness, I was a hyperactive and unfocused child. By contrast, my exceptionally talented sister—seven years my senior—seemed to excel at pretty much everything. I must have been such a disappointment in comparison to her constant and enumerable successes, or at least that's how it felt growing up.

"Damnit, boy. Why can't you get right?" he would sputter at me, pipe smoke spilling from his blackened teeth.

But alas, despite my efforts to quash the loud and rambunctious little boy within, I could never seem to "get right," as it were, and inevitably found myself running into the loving embrace of my supportive and doting grandmother. I don't want to paint the man with too harsh a brush, though. He was not abusive or anything, but he was a hard man reminiscent of a hard time. Strangely, to the outside world, he was charismatic and enjoyable. Most people said he reminded them of Sheriff Taylor on the *Andy Griffith's Show*. But to those of us closest to him, he was often coarse and abrupt if things were not to his liking. Certainly, he loved us, but he had such a strange way of showing it. After all, it was he who taught me to shoot and fish, gifted me my first car, and even poured my first drink. But it had to be on *his* terms, everything done precisely to *his* specifications. Sadly, I would always seem to fall short of his expectations. Looking back, I think his harsh demeanor was an attempt to prepare us for the callousness of the world as he knew it and, in his own strange way, a sign of love.

Grandma, on the other hand, was an absolute saint. For as hard as Grandpa was, Grandma was every bit the warm and loving soul. Quick with a hug, she was always there to wipe our tears and rock us to sleep. She was tender and graceful, patient, humble and charitable—everything that a good woman should be. At the risk of seeming blasphemous, when

I think of the blessed Virgin Mary, it is Grandma's face that I see in my mind. The greatest thing Grandpa ever did was to marry her.

Perhaps things could have been different for him. I don't know much about his childhood, and he never saw fit to discuss it with us. Maybe he was kind and gentle during his youth. Perhaps he even could have grown into a gentle and loving man, but his dang flat feet would forever change the course of his life, laying the foundation for the massive stone walls he built up over a lifetime around his heart. As a boy, he lived with his younger brother on a farm in the middle of nowhere several miles outside Tulsa, Oklahoma. I like to imagine that he might have been like me, energetic and precocious, always looking for adventure. The slow, dull pace of life—which in his later years he would grow to enjoy—was almost unbearable for an impatient young man who was keen on making a mark on the world. As fate would have it, an opportunity arose for him to leave his hometown and start his life as a man.

In the summer of 1943, Grandpa turned eighteen and graduated high school. And about as fast as you would expect, he and his friends raced off to the recruiter's station to enlist. America had been fighting in WWII for almost two years and they were eager to join the fight to get their licks in before all the action was over. But to his dismay, those damned flat feet were just too much for Uncle Sam and Grandpa was not allowed to enlist.

He was devastated. Everything he had been working towards for years was for nothing. Of course, he was happy for his friends and wished them well as they embarked on this exciting journey. But it crushed him to stay behind. Still wanting to serve, he got a job as a highway patrolman. If his friends were fighting to protect the world, he could at least protect their home while they were away. But even the sharp blue uniform of the patrolman was a poor substitute for the drab green of Army fatigues. Deep down, he felt ashamed for not being "in the fight" with his friends. The weeks grew into months, and the months stretched into years. Before long it seemed as though all his friends had gone. Even his younger brother,

Jim—for whom my dad is named—enlisted and served in the 82nd Airborne Division. Everyone was fighting. Everyone except for him.

Before long, the voices of self-doubt in his mind seemed to manifest into the world around him—sideways looks from the teller at the bank whose son was in Normandy, or whispers from a group of girls at the diner whose brothers were at sea. Newspapers, rallies, blood drives. Everywhere he looked was a reminder. Everything and everyone, whether purposeful or not, real or imagined, seemed to judge him constantly. So, to protect his wounded pride, he hardened himself to the world around.

Eventually, the survivors returned home. The streets filled with parades and celebrations. Unquestionably, he was thrilled to reunite with his family and friends who made it home. He thanked God for returning his brother and for bringing the war to an end. But even as the celebrations ended and life seemed to return to normal, nothing was left untouched by the war. In every place and every person, in every conversation, there echoed a memory of the devastating war just beneath the surface. And so, there was no escape for him from the constant reminder that when others went, he stayed home. In response, the imaginary protective walls he had built around his heart grew even higher, and the man became tougher.

My first memory of Grandpa saying something genuinely kind to me was after I reached middle school. In a few short years, I had grown rather dramatically. Seemingly overnight the wiry, energetic boy who irritated him like some persistent gnat, miraculously transformed into a sizable, muscular young man. I began gaining local prominence for my newfound athletic abilities. As I became more focused and goal-oriented, I started gaining recognition both in the classroom as well as on the field. I was even selected as the state's "Student Athlete" award recipient. It seemed to me as though an invisible switch had flipped and Grandpa's attitude towards me completely changed.

In truth, he had warmed to me over the course of a few years. Grandma had always been his conduit to the rest of the world, tempering his brashness with love and compassion. Unfortunately, she passed away unexpectedly from a brain aneurysm when I was nine. She was in church, believe it or not. She had just finished giving the scripture reading, as she did on regular occasion, but this time fumbled several of the words and kept losing her place. It was odd, they thought, because she was normally so sharp. *Oh well, she must be having an off day.* She came back to her seat, said she felt tired, and leaned over on Grandpa's shoulder to rest her eyes. But she never woke up. She died as she had lived, a picture of peace and beauty.

It was hard for everyone, but especially Grandpa. He grew increasingly more aware of what an important role Grandma played in his life, specifically with respect to her ability to mediate between him and the world. A lifetime of barriers had mostly cut him off from the rest of the population, and she had been the lone tether keeping him connected. But with her gone, he felt isolated and alone. Slowly, for the first time in many years, he began reaching out to curb the loneliness. When we would come to visit, he started to take me out on his boat, just the two of us. He would wake me up before the sun and we'd sneak off to check the fishing lines. No longer a child, I had learned to remain silent when we were together. Ironically, it was in this silence that we started to communicate and appreciate each other. With a subtle motion of his head, he would nod approval as I brought in a catch. Occasionally, whenever he found something especially pleasing, he would even grumble a "not bad" as pipe smoke rolled from his maw like an ancient dragon.

As I continued to grow, so too did our relationship. The cold, hard façade seemed to crack ever so slightly, and I began to learn the man within. Our vocabulary grew beyond simple grunts and nods as we started to talk substantively about our thoughts on various issues. Interestingly, I found that most of our beliefs aligned, or at least, on the important things. On the small issues which we failed to agree, mini-intellectual battles would erupt with each of us stubbornly entrenched in our corners, fighting for our views. In a peculiar way, these disagreements further earned me his favor for standing my ground.

We began spending much more time together. When we had the opportunity to visit, instead of being relegated to the house to play with children's toys, Grandpa started having me accompany him on his daily rounds at the farm. I learned how to plow fields and pick crops. He taught me to ride a horse and work in his woodshop. In the early mornings he would take me on his boat to check the fishing lines and in the evening, we would practice shooting. As I would lay down for bed, he would tell me stories about how he and Grandma had traveled the world. He even promised to take me on an adventure one day. And he did. For my fourteenth birthday, he took me to Mexico—just me and him. I remember he arranged for a special dinner for us at a tequila plantation, overlooking the agave fields. That was the night when he bought me my first beer, which was immediately followed by my first shot of tequila. He still had random outbursts of anger, but they seemed tempered and less piercing. Over those years, his icy, guarded demeanor began to fade, and we became rather close in our own way.

But that was nothing compared to after I was accepted into West Point. It was a done deal—I was permanently in his good graces. For maybe the first time ever, he was perpetually smiling. Everywhere we went he would dote and brag on me with increasing absurdity. Even before I started attending the academy, he began publicly referring to me as "the General." He was so darn proud and took every opportunity to tell me so. The first time he saw me in uniform, his eyes welled with tears for a moment before he could repress the flare-up and spit out an approving grumble. He even stood up—which in his old age was a feat—to shake my hand and demand we share a drink.

Over the next few years, I matriculated into the academy and began the process of becoming an Army officer. It was an exciting time as my life began to blossom with new possibilities and adventures. I made lifelong friends, I grew into a man, and I even met the woman who would later become my wife. Truly, it was an amazing chapter in my life. Things for Grandpa, however, took a turn for the worse. I cannot remember a time where Grandpa had been without his pipe. It was like an extension of his body. But a lifetime of smoking and drinking had finally caught up to him. Aside from just being in poor health, his lungs, black and sticky with tar, had finally become riddled with cancer. Needing full-time care, he moved away from the farm and into an assisted living facility, awaiting the inevitable. It seemed to help for a while, but eventually his condition worsened to the point that even being in a home was not enough.

No one told me when he was admitted into the hospital. It was towards the end of my senior year at the academy. With my studies, graduation, and commissioning, Grandpa demanded that I was not to be burdened by his condition. I had important things to do, damnit, and he'd be tarred before he would let some small matter, such as his failing health, interfere.

Towards the end, things were bad. The family who was there diligently stayed by his bedside, holding his hand as he sputtered and coughed, struggling to breath. The medical staff, seeing there was nothing to do and that this was the end, kept urging to "make him more comfortable," which is just a euphemism for pumping him full of drugs until he peacefully passed away. But always the hard-ass, he disregarded their pleas and instead kept fighting against the darkness. Desperate to be alive for my graduation, he would ask anyone who entered the room "Did he make it? Did he make it?"

In the days before my graduation, when he was still able to talk, he forsook the use of all pain medication because he wanted to be lucid for the event. Too stubborn to die, he endured days of incredible pain just to hold onto this world until I had made it through. I've often asked myself why it mattered to him so much. *Why was it so important to remain alive for my graduation?* In part, like most family members, I think it's because he was so darn proud that he wanted to share in the celebration of my commissioning. But I don't think that is the whole truth.

Upon great reflection, I think this was more about him paying back for what he saw as his own shortcomings. Not able to fight for his country due to something he perceived as his own weakness, he'd set himself to the task of saving his progeny of the same fate. He would ensure his ilk was strong and prepared for the battles of life. As a result, not only his son chose to serve, but now his grandson was reaching what he saw as the height of military excellence. All his callousness, all his meanness had not been in vain. And all the pain he was going through, laying in that hospital bed, grasping to life, was his payment to show he really was tough enough. In his youth, he might have stayed behind as others went off to fight, but now he was the one fighting. Each day was proof that he was strong enough to survive.

Certainly, the specifics of this story are unique to my family. But what amazes me is, as I share the tale with others like yourself, I'm constantly greeted with a sense of immediate understanding. I'm shocked at how this story seems to resonate with you and others like you. It seems that, while we don't all have a flat-footed grumpy grandpa, we do all carry some family baggage. Each of us has a misunderstood loved one who tragically seems at odds with the world. We feel lost or confused at their actions, maybe having never had the opportunity to reconcile. Perhaps this is you.

Perhaps you too find yourself tethered to a seemingly unloving relative, never able to meet their expectations. Or perhaps you can't understand why that person, who you so desperately try to please, never seems able to express their love and appreciation in the way you so desperately need. It is possible that, indeed, they are every bit the callous, uncaring ass you think them to be. But it is equally, if not more possible that they are misunderstood, that they love you more than you could possibly know and that you don't have the full context of the life that has led to their present circumstances. As you parse through the past, you begin to understand how your story began long before you arrived.

Forgiveness and empathy are the keys to understanding the depth of these individual's love for you. It wasn't until I began raising my own children that I began to appreciate all that my grandpa did for us. Often, I find remnants of his ghost, echoed in my own actions. Not in his meanness or callousness, but in his conviction and drive for excellence. I see myself pushing my children, in my own way, to go beyond my limits to achieve even more, not out of vanity but out of love. In that same way, you must see the very human person of your loved one, struggling to overcome their own baggage as they strive to serve you with the best guidance possible. Ultimately, whatever their faults, you must know that, despite their inability to always show it, they love you more that you could possibly imagine.

When finally, I walked across the graduation stage and threw my hat in the air, my dad rushed in to take a picture with his flip phone and text it to our relatives back in Oklahoma. Upon receiving the message, our relatives ran in to Grandpa's hospital room exclaiming that I had graduated and held up a grainy picture of me in my uniform proudly holding up my diploma. Beneath the picture my father had typed a short message to his own father, the last thing he would ever communicate to his dad. The message read, "He made it!" For a long time, Grandpa just sat there looking at the picture. Then, clutching the photo to his chest, he smiled, laid his head back on his hospital bed and passed on.

Like Grandpa's role in my life, all our stories are filled with a cast of characters who shape and influence you. There is a past, stretching back generations, which has led to this moment. With every new page you write in your story, you continue their legacy, proudly driving towards a greater tomorrow. But you don't have to do it alone.

16 ···· CHIPS & SALSA

"Death cannot stop true love. All it can do is delay it for a while." –
Westley, The Princess Bride

My best friend in college was a girl. She was intelligent and funny, passionate and caring. It was only by complete coincidence that she also happened to be a total smoke show. If I had to describe how I felt about her then in a single word, it would be: buddy. And if I had to describe that younger version of me in a single word, it would be: idiot. How could I be so freaking dense that I didn't realize that I was hopelessly, unmistakably in love with her.

Her name was Anita Salas, but everybody called her "Salsa." Nicknames are a big part of Army culture, so it was common to snag yourself a moniker. You just hoped it wasn't for doing something stupid. One of the guys had his mom mail him a picture of his cat, and to this day everyone still calls him "Whiskers." Salsa was much more fortunate. Her Hispanic roots and spicy wit made the anagram too tempting to resist. In fact, the alias fit her so well that most people never thought to ask about her real name. Albeit I found all this out much later. When we first met, we didn't even speak.

Though we were assigned to the same company, meaning that we lived in the same barracks area, we did not meet in earnest until swimming class. As Plebes (first-year cadets), we were not allowed to speak outside of our rooms, so there was little opportunity to interact. Luckily, she was assigned as my swim lane partner for the duration of the class. I was thrilled to have the opportunity to become better acquainted. After all, it is always good to build relationships with your company mates. The fact that she looked mighty fine in her Army-issued one-piece bathing suit had absolutely nothing to do with it. Well, okay, maybe it mattered a *little*.

During our first assignment, we were instructed to swim from one side of the pool to the other in as few strokes as possible. As a young, hormone-fueled teenage boy, I—and pretty much every other guy in the room—immediately went to work trying to impress her.[4] I had served as a lifeguard for several years and felt confident in my abilities. We all hopped into the pool and began to swim to the other side, each of us thrusting forward with all our might. One by one, we emerged from the other end. Around the room, all the guys started shouting out their stroke counts as they climbed out of the water.

"Ten!" called out a tall, lanky guy at the far side of the pool.

"I did nine!" exclaimed another.

"Me too," someone else joined in.

With a grin, I listed off my stroke count for the class.

"Eight," I stated proudly.

A few people rolled their eyes, but most gave signs of congratulations. Small competitions like these filled our lives as cadets, and we were used to the good-natured rivalries.

---

[4] As I came to realize throughout my relationship with Salsa, at no time did any of this "jack-assery" impress her. In fact, it had quite the opposite effect.

"What about her?" inquired the lanky guy. "What'd she get?"

All the commotion stopped as we turned to hear her answer. She looked up to meet our stares.

"Six," she stated coolly, without any sense of boastfulness.

After that, I made it a point to talk to her during class. With the ice broken, we found that the conversation between us flowed easily, and we quickly became best friends. During any free time between classes or in the evenings, I would swing by her room to hang out. She was different from anyone I had ever met. She was every bit as funny and easygoing as my guy friends. But unlike my "bros," we never felt like we needed to boast or compete. We just clicked. It also helped that we both were still dating our significant others from high school. With any romantic possibilities off the table, there wasn't any pressure to try and impress her or "spit game," like I often felt with other girls. I could just be myself. Ironically, it was this lack of trying that allowed us to become so tremendously close.

We started hanging out pretty much all the time. Even though we were not allowed to talk outside, we would still walk to class together. With subtle hand gestures and facial movements, we would pass silly secret messages as we walked. Almost like some form of telepathy, we could communicate whole conversations comprised of these imperceptive non-verbal cues. In the evenings, we would help each other with homework and complain about the woes of being a Plebe. And on the rare occasion we were allowed off-post privileges (OPPs), we would spend the time exploring the neighboring towns—perusing old shops, going apple picking, or maybe having a picnic in a park. It really didn't matter the activity; it was all just an excuse to spend time together.

It wasn't long before people started to notice we were always around each other. I even earned myself an accompanying moniker. Since we were together so often, it made sense that our nicknames should also coincide. Thus, I became *Chips*.

As you can imagine, there were a few lame jokes and innuendos from our friends, but we didn't care because we knew it was all in good fun. They were young, immature, and—most importantly—jealous. *But they shouldn't be*, I thought. We had a completely platonic, non-romantic friendship. No big deal. After all, we were both still very committed to our respective long-distance relationships, which had been going on for over a year. As we entered West Point, we each believed wholeheartedly that we would ultimately end up with our boyfriend or girlfriend after graduation.

But as time progressed, our conviction to those relationships began to wane. While we endured the grueling demands of West Point life, our significant others were enjoying the fun-filled delights of civilian college. The constant barrage of drunken late-night phone calls and incessant social drama began to take its toll. Somehow, the distance between us was no longer purely geographical. There is a reason why the "two percent club" exists.[5] So, sharing the same frustrations, Salsa and I would slip away to commiserate. As our hometown relationships continued to weaken, we found our bond with each other growing ever stronger as we hung out more and more.

One early summer night, we found ourselves at a local landmark, Trophy Point. Besides being outside the cadet area, affording us the opportunity to talk freely, it is also one of the most beautiful landscapes in the world. From this location you can see the tranquil Hudson River meandering endlessly to the horizon, banked by stately mountains stretching to a cloudless blue sky. It was majestic.

We sat there for hours, talking and laughing. And as day turned to night and the sun began to sink into the shining Hudson Valley, I was struck by how beautiful she was in the golden light of the fading summer

---

[5] The "two percent club" refers to the fact that, statistically, only 2 percent of people entering West Point in a relationship will maintain that relationship until graduation.

sun. Unintentionally, I found myself scooting closer to her on the bench. *Dang, she smells good, too*, I thought as the scent of her hair wafted up on the sweet summer breeze. In the growing darkness we locked eyes, an electricity surging between us. As fireflies began to chirp their lights proudly around us, I could just make out the shape of her lips. I could feel my palms grow sweaty as I inched them towards her on the bench. Again, we grew closer; this time she was the one moving in. Our eyes met each other as we lingered in the moment. For what seemed like forever, we sat there frozen, both too afraid of our feelings to move.

Bang! Bang! Bang!

Three sharp blasts rang out through the night as a car roared past us. At first, I thought we were in the middle of a drive-by shooting. Images from *The Godfather* raced through my mind as my brain tried to catch up and piece together what the hell was happening. Prior to this incident, I'd like to think I would have reacted like they do in stories, heroically jumping in front of the damsel to save her from harm. But none of that happened. It all took place so fast. I jumped up, but stood there, frozen like an idiot.

As my mind was racing, it occurred to me that for the second time that night, I was rendered a prisoner within my motionless and unyielding body. I felt a gust of wind as the car barreled past, no more than a few feet from where we stood. Then, with an abrupt and wicked forcefulness, the car slammed into a tree only a few yards from where we stood. Shattered glass and tattered metal flew into the sky as a ball of flame erupted from under the hood. It was like a scene from an action movie. But here, in the real world on this beautiful summer night, it was so out of place that I simply couldn't accept what was happening. The pieces just would not fit.

All this took place in less than a second. As my conscious mind frantically caught up, I started to understand what had happened. For some unknown reason, a car had been flying out of control across the open field to our rear. The loud *bangs* were a consequence of the rampaging car crashing into a series of small decorative cannons which lined the road. Unencumbered by their presence, the car charged onward until its final battle with a tree. We stood for a moment, surveying the wreckage, when something stirred from within the now smoke-filled cab.

"The driver!" we yelled in unison as the realization suddenly struck us.

Without saying another word, we rushed, side by side, towards the vehicle. As we ran to the nearest door, we could see the driver on the other side slumped over and unmoving in his seat. I called to him but he didn't answer. Blood was trickling down the side of his head. I tried to open the passenger door, but it had been damaged beyond repair and refused to budge. After a brief, futile last tug at the handle, I ran around to the other side. By the time I had made my way around and opened the driver's door, Salsa, recognizing that only one of us would be able to fit into the cab, wasted no time and was already on the phone with the police. All that time silently communicating enabled us to work seamlessly without the need for words. We both understood what needed to happen and, reading the other's movements, instantly delineated responsibility.

Moreover, because we both had complete confidence in each other, we did not have to waste time checking on what the other was doing. She was doing her job, now I needed to do mine, and I needed to do it fast. There weren't any flames inside the cab yet, but you could feel the heat radiating from behind the dash. Smoke was now steadily leaking out from all the vents. Right away, I tried to pull the man from the car, but his seatbelt—ironically designed to save his life—trapped him inside the burning car. It took only a moment to find the buckle for the seatbelt, but my hands were shaking so badly from the nerves that I couldn't push the latch.

I took a breath and recited the mantra known to all soldiers, "slow is smooth, and smooth is fast." Pushing down the animalistic urge to freak out and run away, I calmly pressed the release and the seatbelt relented. It took only a moment for me to lean the man's torso over and pull him from the car, headfirst. I started dragging him away from the car and began looking for a safe patch to lay him down. I was surprised to find that the guy didn't seem that heavy. *Must be the adrenaline*, I thought, remembering the tales of mothers lifting cars off their babies. Then I turned back around and realized Salsa was carrying his legs while still talking on the phone.

Of course she was.

Right away, we got to work doing an injury assessment. Both of us had served as lifeguards throughout our time in high school, not to mention all the military training we had received to become Combat Life Savers (CLS), and rapidly began walking through the steps.

"Check his breathing," she reminded me, and then went back to talking with the 911 operator.

I knelt, placed my face over his, and turned my head, hoping to see his chest move or feel his breath on my cheek. Nothing. I looked up, wide-eyed, to see Salsa staring back with the same expression. All this seemed so much easier with the plastic practice dummies. A few seconds passed between us, and then I again placed my cheek next to his lips, hoping for some sign of life. Again, nothing.

Pull it together, I thought, *you know what to do*. Immediately, I moved into position to start CPR. Stiff armed, I placed the heel of my palms over the man's chest and began to thrust downward like we had practiced so many times. With a sickening *crack*, I could feel his ribs buckle and break beneath my weight. Following each compression, I shouted out the count, growing louder and more determined with each repetition. Then, after reaching thirty, I blew a few breaths into his lungs and repeated the cycle. Over and over, we kept the pattern—push, push, push, breathe. Salsa knelt beside me to assist and keep me focused. By this point, a few other cadets saw the commotion and rushed over to help, but I didn't notice.

Push, push, push, breathe, I continued.

It had to work. It *had* to work.

At one point, the man seemed to take in a few breaths on his own and even started to mumble. A glimmer of hope grew inside us. But that hope was short-lived as the man slipped back into unconsciousness.

Exhausted, I let one of the other cadets take over the compressions as I moved on to address the bleeding. Oh lord, there was so much blood. *How had I not noticed it before?* On the ground, on my hands, on my clothes. It was everywhere. That's when I saw the huge gash in the side of the man's head where a fragment of his skull protruded outward. *How could we have not seen this until now?* We continued to administer CPR, but by that point, it was futile. Everyone could see the truth—the man was dead. I stayed lost in that realization for a long time.

He's dead. He's dead.

The words echoed and swirled around like a haze in my mind. Then, coming out of the miasma, I could feel Salsa place her hand on my shoulder. That is when I noted, for the first time, that a fleet of ambulances and police cars had arrived on the scene, their red and blue lights illuminating the landscape.

It was over.

The authorities would handle everything from here. The complete anarchy and destruction that had burst into our lives and consumed our entire universe for the previous half hour was at an end.

The next thing to happen was, in its own way, outrageous. Certainly, it pales in comparison to the tragedy that we had just witnessed. Still, what we did next continues to shock and amaze me to this day. Realizing that it was late and nearing Lights Out (aka bedtime for soldiers), we fled the scene and ran back to our rooms. We did not talk to the police, we didn't follow up with the paramedics, we just ran back to our rooms. Our little Plebe brains had been so deeply conditioned to fear any form of tardiness that we seriously thought we might get in trouble for being late. The thought of staying didn't even occur to us as an option. A man had, quite literally, died in my arms and "missing taps" was foremost on my mind.

We never did learn the man's name, or the full truth as to why he drove his car at full speed into a tree. Later, we discovered that he was a groundskeeper in his late fifties. Was it suicide or an accident? To this day, we still don't know. But there was nothing we could have done to save him. The following days were relatively uneventful. We showed up for formation, went to class, did our duties, and kept up with the usual cadet routine. Weirdly, it never occurred to us that we should tell anyone about the events of that night. And, other than some seriously strange looks from one sleepy, bleary-eyed cadet as I ran through the hallway covered in blood, no one seemed to notice anything had happened. For the most part, Salsa and I just kept to ourselves, privately working through the emotional trauma.

The day following the accident, I broke up with my girlfriend. She had called to talk about some new drama within her sorority and I just couldn't pretend to care for another second. It was over. We were finished. It was time to pull the plug. I might not have been positive what I wanted in a significant other, but she sure as hell wasn't it. I spent the next few weeks wrestling with this question. What *did* I want in a partner? I had expended the better part of my youth bouncing between relationships exactly like the one which had just ended. I was still young, only nineteen at the time, and had only seriously dated a handful of girls. But they were all pretty similar. I always assumed I had a *type* and was destined to end up with someone with those same qualities. But something had changed, and I found the idea of spending another moment in one of those relationships utterly detestable.

Such a big part of adolescence is trying to find our place in the world. The infinite possibilities are exciting but can also be overwhelming. Now, amidst that chaos and endless possibilities, find your soulmate. Out of the 7.8 billion people on the planet, find that one perfect person who is your exact match. If only you can find the one person out there who fits you flawlessly, then you can ride off into the sunset and live happily ever after. Such a task seems hopeless. Like Sylvia Plath and her great fig tree from *The Bell Jar*, we stand there paralyzed by the endless array of options. We're too afraid to pick, because choosing one means that you forsake the rest. So, we end up standing there like a bunch of idiots, gaping on at a stupid metaphorical fig tree for our whole lives while we look for just the right one.

I've got hard news for you. That perfect person—that unique match that fits together seamlessly with you and only you—that Instagram fairytale ending … it doesn't exist. You have been told a lie. We're convinced that when you find your special person everything falls into place and your relationship flows effortlessly. But that's simply not true. Imagine you had a ceramic bowl that was broken in two. And then you found a room full of other half broken bowls. It doesn't matter how many fragments you try to match against your own, none will be an exact fit. Of course, some may work better than others, but you can never fully repair the damage that has been done to your vessel. The same is true for our relationships. All of us, including you, are broken. And as such, you will never be able to find someone who matches your cracks exactly. So, does that mean we give up, that we shouldn't even bother looking? Of course not! Just because there is no perfect match, doesn't mean there aren't good matches out there, some much better than others. But no matter who you choose, there requires tremendous work and sacrifice as you sand down your edges and give of yourselves to each other.

There's an ancient Japanese art called Kinsukuroi that centers on mending broken pottery. Instead of trying to hide the cracks and restore the bowl to its original state, they embrace a new vision and bind the pieces together with something beautiful like gold. Yes, the artist must sacrifice the original autonomy of the bowl, but the final splendor far surpasses anything the starting piece could have hoped to be. In this same way, you must give of yourself, giving up your pride and vanity. Each day, you must sacrifice yourself to your partner in endless service. Move beyond the fickle, selfishness of infatuation. When you ask, "Why do you want to be with that person?" the answer should not be "They make me so happy" or "I love the way they make me feel." Notice that both these sentiments are focused on *you*.

Instead, you want to be able to answer the question with, "I want to take care of them forever" and "I want to protect them and keep them safe." Now, find someone who will give themselves to you in the same way. Instead of spending all your emotional energy on looking for that exact perfect fit, find someone who will hold your hand as they go through the fire with you to forge your pieces together in an eternal bond. Just as a finished Kinsukuroi is far more beautiful than the original, a romantic bond built on hard work, sacrifice, and commitment is immeasurably more glorious.

So, what do you want? I asked myself. I wanted someone I could count on. I wanted someone I respected. I wanted someone who, without batting an eye, would run by my side towards a burning car. I wanted … her name rang out like a siren in my head. I jumped up from my chair and ran to Salsa's room to tell her my revelation. Sprinting down the hall, I caught a glimpse of a few upperclassmen casting stern glances in my direction. But I was a man on a mission, and nothing was going to stop me. The door to her room was open, so I gave the customary knock and rushed in. That is when I realized she was in the process of hanging up the phone. With a swift motion, she jammed the phone back into its base a bit too hard. Something was off. She seemed unhappy. Before I could open my mouth to speak, she looked up somberly.

"I just broke up with my boyfriend." A small sigh escaped her lips.

"Oh, no. That sucks," I responded, trying to sound solemn as a small grin peeked out of the corner of my mouth and betrayed my true feelings.

Two months later, we were dating.

Three years later, we were married.

Without question, I am a better man because of my wife. She tempers my anger and softens my edges when I am frustrated. She acknowledges and celebrates the work I do to provide for our family. She inspires me to take on new challenges and encourages me along the way. Each day she grinds through the business and logistics of family life so that I can focus my efforts on guiding the direction of our household. She has gifted me with two beautiful children, a welcoming and peaceful home, and an affectionate and love-filled life. And most of all, through her quiet example, she has led me to a fuller relationship with God.

I can't tell you how important it is to have someone in your corner, a spouse that will always, *always* be there. Even in your worst moments, such as when you are frustrated with work, worried about the future, and not acting like your best self to those you love, they are there. They are there because you are two parts made into one. That connection is, aside from your relationship with the Almighty, the single most important thing in your life. It is from these relationships that you have the foundation to do all other things. It is this love that brings forth children and all the adventures of family. It is this joy that renews and makes you stronger each day. It is this safety and steadfastness that gives you the courage to persevere even in the hardest of times. My professional confidence, my peacefulness, my purpose, and my devotion are all things sprung from the holy waters of my marriage.

Be courageous enough to give yourself completely to another. This does not mean each moment will be filled with happiness—a fleeting rush of endorphins. But such a commitment is the route to great and lasting joy. Anything of worth has a price and requires sacrifice. This axiom holds true for not just relationships, but for all of life. Have no doubts, there will be challenging times ahead. Your story will have ups, and I promise you, it will have some devastating downs. But do not fret. Celebrate these hardships as a prelude to great success. Like a rainbow after a ranging storm, the most beautiful moments in life often come at the heels of our greatest challenges.

17 ···· THE MOON TREE

"Long is the way and hard, that out of Hell leads up to the light." –
John Milton, Paradise Lost

We had been in the rain for about seventy-two hours. The freak Missouri storm raged down unforgivingly and I half-expected Noah to show up and start shepherding us onto his ark, two by two. Before stepping off, we ensured everyone had the prescribed wet weather gear from the packing list, but at this point, it didn't really matter—we were soaked to the bone. Only one more training event remained for this particular cycle of Basic Combat Training (BCT). The Night Infiltration Course, or as we liked to call it "NIC at night," was easily the most challenging and memorable event of a soldier's initial training. In a simulated combat environment, trainees must complete a hundred-meter low crawl while live bullets are fired over their heads.

Like every event conducted in BCT, a ridiculous number of precautions were emplaced to ensure the safety of everyone involved.

Doing NIC was probably safer than driving into work every morning. But the trainees don't know that. As far as they were concerned, we might as well have been charging up Hamburger Hill … which was kind of the point.

Because of the developmental and emotional significance of the event, the Drill Sergeants and I took care to ensure it was a special and impactful occasion. Though not required, we would always integrate the NIC at the climax of a weeklong Field Training Exercise (FTX). This helped to elevate the magnitude of the drill by contextualizing it amidst the hardships of the preceding week. Each FTX varied slightly, since we gave different drill sergeants the opportunity to lead the planning process, but they typically consisted of a twenty-kilometer road march, various tasks and battle drills, and patrol base operations. But whatever the scenario, the climax was always conducting this assault on an enemy location while under fire.

Besides the obvious training benefits, NIC also helped to forge a connection and respect for our courageous brothers and sisters throughout history. It is one thing to hear about the heroism of American troops—such as the assaults made on the beaches of Normandy. But by crawling through mud and sand yourself, over huge distances, you gain a better appreciation for the incredible feats accomplished by our brethren. Moreover, as a long-time staple of BCT, it was one of those events that draws all soldiers—young and old—together over this shared suck-fest.

Immediately following this physically and emotionally taxing exercise, we conducted a special event called the Values Tag Ceremony, to drive home the importance of the moment. This sacred ritual marked the official transformation from trainee to soldier. Gathered around a massive bonfire, we celebrated the completion of training and award special dog tags emblazoned with the Army values to those who had earned the right to call themselves a part of the Profession of Arms:

loyalty, duty, respect, selfless service, honor, integrity and personal courage.

The ceremony was an incredibly powerful moment in the development of a soldier. Leaders went to great lengths to ensure everything was perfectly crafted to create the proper ambiance and set the right tone for the event. At that point in my command, we'd already flawlessly conducted four or five of these occasions and the process was fairly ironed out. However, this specific instance did not go as smoothly. It had been raining for three days when we began the long foot march to the training site. Like all military operations, bad weather was always challenging; but that situation was especially treacherous. Not only had the rains been unyielding, but the temperature had also dropped dramatically and unexpectedly as we prepared to execute NIC. As the soldiers marched onward, we heard the soft crunch of their boots on the newly formed ice.

As a leader, it is important to constantly balance the need to accomplish the mission with the well-being of your soldiers. Obviously, you do not want to be the guy that runs back home at the first signs of adversity. We're in the business of making tough-as-nails steely-eyed killers, after all. At the same time, you also don't want to cause half of your people to get frostbite because you are being a hard-ass. Bottom line: it's kind of hard to be a steely-eyed killer if you have hypothermia. Like most leadership challenges, you must find that "baby bear" sweet spot in the middle.

After deliberating with my NCOs and analyzing the situation, I decided we would remain in the field, but implement some additional mitigation to make sure people didn't freeze. With only a few hours remaining, it seemed like a minor tragedy to stop just short of the finish line. Nevertheless, we rapidly coordinated for special heaters and tents to be set up in our staging area to ensure there weren't any cold-weather injuries. With the new plan in place, we marched onward, as my XO led the effort getting all the equipment set up for our arrival.

By the time we finished the trek uphill to the assembly area, the temperature had dropped well below freezing. Our heads were snow whipped, and our boots, clothes, and water in our CamelBaks had turned to ice. Despite our extra precautions, it was absolutely brutal, and I could tell that even the most seasoned members of our cadre were starting to wear down.

Had I made the right call?

Had things been any worse, I'm not sure we would have made it without issue. But thanks to the grace of God and the constant supervision of my incredible drill sergeant team, we were able to make it without any major issues. Rapidly, we began cycling platoons through the warming tents as we conducted our final rehearsals and prepared for our assault on the objective at NIC. Immediately, we had everyone swapping out their cold wet clothes for the drier clothes tucked away in their rucks (Apparently, all the wet-weather bags the drill sergeants had been harping on for all those weeks came in handy—shocking!).

Cadre walked around the tents, making sure everyone was safe and dry. Slowly, we started to see life flowing back into the troops as they warmed up. And as soon as that happened, it was time to get to work. After a much too quick respite in the warming tents, we headed out to complete the training mission. Under the cover of darkness, we moved through the woods into our Objective Rally Point (ORP) and staged for the simulated attack. The site was set atop a large hill, which, during more pleasant weather, offered a serene and picturesque view of the surrounding area. But that night, the climb seemed to last forever as we clawed our way up the windy, ice-covered slope.

Panting heavily with the exertion of the climb, we finally reached the top and took our position. Our clothes, newly drenched in sweat, again began to turn to ice. Freezing rain continued to shoot down like icy needles, stinging our faces with each drop. Whatever warmth had been renewed at the assembly area was leached again from our bodies.

Miserable but focused, we silently waited for the designated time. The dense foliage provided a slight reprieve from the biting wind and icy downpour, but not by much. Looking around, we could see small groups of soldiers huddled together as they fought to stave off the cold. Plumes of steam arose from their huddled masses. Finally, the clock struck 2100 and I gave the command to begin the faux attack.

With a sharp *tweeeeeeet*, I blew my whistle, giving the signal to begin. Soldiers rushed to scale the barrier wall and started the final climb to the objective. The staccato bursts of *tat tat tat* rang out in the night as bullets raced a few feet overhead, every fifth round burning bright like a meteor. Around us, simulated artillery fire exploded in a shower of sparks and flame. Like a perverse Disney ride, everything was especially crafted to transport the individual to a place where they forgot the reality of the situation. Everyone—including the cadre—could have easily lost themselves in the chaos and, for however briefly, believed they were in genuine combat.

Slowly and painfully, through the ice and snow and sand, we pushed ourselves forward. Through tunnels, over obstacles, and under barbed wire, we crawled; those short hundred-meters seemed to stretch on for an eternity. Eventually, mercifully, we made it to the end. As each soldier crossed the proverbial "finish line" they formed into small teams, cleared one of the buildings on the objective, and moved to the final assembly area. Once everyone was safely accounted for, and the standard post-range procedures were conducted, we started our movement back down the hill towards our initial rally point. Drill sergeants circulated through the troops as we marched, checking to ensure everyone was okay. Even as cold and wet as we were, each step down the hill lifted our spirits higher.

At the base of the hill, about a half-mile away, we could see a large bonfire beginning to pierce through the darkness, the first site of the long-awaited Values Tag Ceremony symbolizing that their hardship was drawing to a close. It was finished.

They had done it.

With a wave of emotion, trainees started to realize that the hardship of BCT was over. Reinvigorated by this realization, our pace quickened as we marched toward the blaze. The cold seemed to disappear as soldiers again found themselves marching with purpose—peppy and excited for the coming ceremony. In isolation, you would have had no idea that only a few moments prior these young warriors were near exhaustion. Like ancient Roman centurions returning home from a victory, they paraded down the road and around the fire.

In my two years as a commander, I conducted many of these rituals, but none compared to that night. Amidst the bleak, cold backdrop of that harsh winter storm I witnessed utter joy, utter triumph. New soldiers sang cadences, bellowing out with pride into the crisp, cold night air. Drill sergeants shared stories of their own experiences in combat and lessons they had learned throughout their careers. We laughed and celebrated as we welcomed these trainees into our profession as brothers and sisters.

Then, as though the spirit of this camaraderie permeated into the air around us, the wind and snow yielded. The night grew silent, and the air grew thick and warm, like a comforting blanket settling around us. Something about the moment felt different—it felt otherworldly and magical. So much so, that everyone fell silent. You could hear the soft rustle of leaves in the distance as a gentle breeze brushed against our cheeks, interrupted only by the playful crackling of the fire. Magic was in the air. From behind the clouds, a hidden full moon, glorious and shining, emerged from the horizon to smile down rays of silver. In its path, standing alone atop the hill from where we had just returned stood a giant gnarled old oak. Even from this distance, you could make out the twisted, knotted trunk, jutting out with a million bony limbs. Like an ancient old warrior, he stood wise and noble.

How many nights had this old tree witnessed? How many ceremonies had he presided over, looking on with nobility as hundreds of thousands of soldiers paraded before him? In the darkness and confusion of the night, we had not noticed him. In fact, I had *never* noticed him. But tonight, he saw fit to reveal himself to us, stretching out his ethereal arms in solute. Almost like the Almighty had sent a personal emissary to watch over and assure us from his majestic and stately perch. It was *magnificent*.

The hellish ice storm, which had been our bane only minutes prior, had dressed the tree in perfect, clear ice. As though fully encapsulated, trunk to twig, in crystal, the tree began to glisten in the light of the moon. It was as if angels had hung a million jewels from every branch—it was breathtaking. The warm, heavenly glow of the shimmering tree juxtaposing the harshness of the world around us created a piece of living art the likes of which I had never seen. No one spoke or even moved, too afraid the slightest noise would somehow break the tree's magical hold. We all just stood for a few moments basking in the outrageous beauty of that instant. By some cosmic fortune, some incredible serendipity, we were privileged to share in this perfect moment. It was as if everything had been building up to this very instant. Somehow all the hardship and training, early mornings and late nights, all the sweat and the tears had simply been a test. And *this* was our reward.

Far too often, we find ourselves wrapped up in the crisis of the moment. Sometimes, in the military, everything is important, needs to be done *now*, and is a dire emergency. We're always moving, always going, faster and faster. Everything is whizzing by so quickly, it's near impossible to even see what is going on around us. In our eagerness to get the job done, we throw ourselves into a knife fight. But if all we are doing is trying to survive, we never have the space to breathe and think. When everything is important … *nothing* is.

We arrive at our most precious life moments only after suffering through an intense crucible. Consider the sunset vista and the end of a long mountain climb. Such a view is always sweeter after having climbed the rocky crag of the mountain's face when compared to simply driving up the paved route to the top. Surely, it is the same view, but one was earned through sweat and toil. You are only able to fully appreciate the context and majesty when you truly understand all that went in to creating it. Such moments are earned through a test of will. They are a gift for your focus and determination. So, embrace hardship because it often leads us to the most glorious moments in life. So many of us find themselves against hardship and turn quickly back. But I implore you to keep pushing forward.

It's like the man wondering through the desert who gives up just before the oasis. Don't give up, you are almost there. Just over that next ridge lays the respite you've been praying for; it is the treasure at the end of the rainbow. Keep going and I promise you will find your glorious moment. And, after all your toil and strife, when one of these perfect moments finally presents itself, stop and soak it in. Relish every instant. Undoubtedly, something new will be tugging at your coat strings and you will feel compelled to the next crisis. Nevertheless, take a breath. Soak in the joy of life; I promise whatever awaits you will still be there when you return.

Just breathe, fully aware of yourself in the present, connecting yourself to all past efforts that led to now and all that will happen in the future as a result. You have found a rose in the desert, respect it as such, for these wonders will not always be there to light your way in the dark times ahead. Moments like these can fly past us if we aren't paying attention. Even if you do manage to not let it slip past, it can be challenging to appreciate these stories within the context of your life. Finding a mentor, someone more experienced who can shed light on your situation, is tremendously helpful when collecting your stories into a cohesive package that assists you in your continued growth.

That night, completely exhausted, we stared on together in silence, relishing in the unspeakable beauty of the moon tree. All the struggles of our adventure were over, all our worries were done, at least for now. The journey to this point had not been an easy one. The grimy, dirt-covered faces of these new soldiers showed joy and relief, having not just overcome the trials of Basic, but having battled the relentless inner-demons of self-doubt. Were they tough enough to become a soldier? Could they handle the immense mental and physical challenges and muster the resolve to keep going? Were they ready to become adults, standing on their own? Could they survive away from the support of their parents to chart their own path, or would they need to run back home to the safety and comfort of their childhood? But now they knew, they knew for certain. They were good enough and strong enough. They *could* make their own way in the world, standing shoulder to shoulder with their brothers and sisters.

But it wasn't just the trainees who seemed renewed and relieved. The drill sergeants, with their unwavering professionalism and incessant call to perfection, had their own battles to fight. The high-speed pace and constant pressures of being in "full drill sergeant" mode took its toll, both physically and mentally. They were tired. Their relationships strained, both at work and at home. Drill tours are only a few years, so they knew it wasn't permanent. But could their families last? Could *they* last? Yes, *yes* they could. Moments such as these washed away doubt and rejuvenated the spirit. It seemed to make all the hardship worth it. They were making a difference.

And then there was me, shouldering the weight of command. I knew we were a team, but ultimately, I had to be the one to make the big decisions, like whether to decide to press on in the cold or to turn back. People depended on me to make the right choice. They needed me to keep them safe, to keep them trained and motivated, to ensure their needs and that of their families were being met. As you will hear over and over, "everything that does or doesn't happen is your responsibility." Couple with this the taboo, but very real, fact that your performance as a company commander is the single most critical aspect when being looked at future success in the military. It's make-or-break and can have a real impact on the next several years, if not the rest of your career. That shit can really mess with your head!

But no, I really was doing well. I had a great team who stuck together and got the job done. I was proud of their work and felt confident in being evaluated next to any of our sister companies. And more important than anything else, I could tell I had the respect of my NCOs. Looking through the crowd, I could see the stalwart faces of my team, each casting a nod of deference in my direction. Somehow, despite my fumbles and mistakes, I'd landed on the right side of the line. They trusted me and that mattered more than I could ever describe. It's a thought I clutched close to my chest, a sacred jewel made all the more precious because I knew one day, I would have to let it go. My time in command would come to an end and fade to a memory. But for the moment, I savored the sweetness and warmth of having been a part of something special.

Cherish these moments that dot the landscape of your life. In the blink of an eye, you'll wake up and these days will be behind you. I know that seems impossible, especially when you are grinding through the endless monotony of life on the front line. But you have only to ask an old fogey and they will tell you the same thing—those long hard nights trudging through the wilderness are some of the best moments of your life. Respect them as such.

On that cold, winter night in the middle-of-nowhere Missouri, huddled around a few hundred new soldiers and my team of drill sergeants, we touched heaven. As if through a tiny pinprick, we glimpsed the smallest fraction of God's infinite love and perfection, and it filled us with peace and hope. Certainly, there would be more fights to come, more trials and tribulations, more rocky roads and uncertainties, but for now we all stared at the tree as it smiled approvingly upon us. Its light shone down upon the new solders, casting its noble approval—a sign of a job well done.

18 ···· MERRY CHRISTMAS, COLONEL CROSS

"Through the years we all will be together if the fates allow" – "Have Yourself a Merry Little Christmas"

The class leaned forward to watch as Colonel Cross turned to the chalkboard to write the new topic of the day. As he pressed the chalk firmly to the board, bits of dust drifted slowly to the ground like snowflakes. Unconsciously, I glanced to the window, boyishly hoping to see real snow fluttering down to create a winter wonderland. The sky was clouded and dark, shrouded in the grey mist that seemed to cover West Point from November until March. It was windy and cold, but alas, no snow. That night was Christmas dinner, my fourth and last time enjoying this special event—and I wanted it to be perfect. Enjoying the festivities with my closest comrades was going to be incredible, no matter what, but the child inside of me yearned for snow. Still, there was time.

I turned back to the front of the class, watching as our professor finished writing and the last bit of flakes wafted down to the ground. I briefly imagined tiny ant-sized cadets making little snow angles in the dust below and a grin spread across my face. Yeah, there's still time for snow.

"Welcome, team," COL Cross joyously bellowed from the front of the class. "I know tonight is the big holiday dinner, so I've got a good one for you today!"

We peered behind him to read "Favorite Christmas Traditions" written in large, freakishly neat handwriting. Some instructors like to jump straight into class, not wanting to waste a single moment as they attempt to cram every second of learning into the allotted time. One of my other instructors would sometimes talk, unbroken, from the start of class to the end, writing feverishly the entire time.

But not COL Cross.

He always liked to ease into things by warming up the class with conversation—hence, the topic of the day. It was good; it felt like he really cared about you individually. Sure, we'd get to the physics, but personally developing each student was more important. He surveyed the room with a wide-mouthed smile, looking each student in the eyes. Some squirmed in their chairs and averted their gaze, not wanting to be the first person called on. It doesn't matter how long you've been in school, there always seems to be an aversion to public speaking early in the morning. Nevertheless, COL Cross was an experienced professor and let the palpable silence linger in the air. As he scanned my area of the class, his eyes locked with mine. The ancient metal and wood desk and chair combo, which decorated our outdated classroom, seemed to grow especially uncomfortable. Rapidly, I scanned through my memories, trying to think of my favorite Christmas tradition. The hint of a smile must have crossed my face and COL Cross jumped at the opportunity.

"So, watcha got for me?" he said, walking over to my desk.

It took just a moment for the memory to solidify.

"Las Posadas," I replied.

Each year, my hometown in Missouri (pronounced Mah-zur-ah by locals) would host a huge festival which stretched from Thanksgiving through Christmas. The entire historic Main Street would transform into an enchanted Victorian winter wonderland, complete with roving carolers, chestnut rosters, and various Santas from around the world. People would come from miles around to enjoy the spectacle. But the climax of the festival was always Las Posadas, Spanish for "The Inns."

Las Posadas follows Mary and Joseph's journey into Bethlehem as they tried to find a place to shelter for the night. Thousands of people would crowd into the narrow, cobblestone streets of my hometown to watch as our Joseph led his pregnant wife atop a donkey to various shops along Main Street, continually asking for a place to stay. But as you probably know, there was never any rooms available. Finally arriving to the town center—newly decorated to look like a manger—the entire town would celebrate the birth of Jesus Christ. Shoulder to shoulder with our neighbors, nestled in the warmth and comradery of the season, we would hold hands around a giant Christmas fire, singing carols into the night. Pure and holy, untarnished by so much of the commercialism of today's world, this special event remains one of my favorite childhood memories. Regaled by my story, COL Cross turned to the class to share his own favorite Christmas tradition.

"Nothing fires me up quite like a good old fashion Christmas card," he announced.

We all chuckled and agreed, recalling our own experiences with the annual family newsletter. But as he elaborated, he explained it was much more than just a yearly announcement. In his estimation, this deliberate effort to remain connected with his friends and colleagues served as a major contributor to both his professional and personal successes. Due to the extremely transient lifestyle of most military personnel, it can be challenging to maintain a lasting connection throughout the years, especially with respected leaders. Many people spend a few years fostering a positive, fruitful relationship with a mentor, only to move and have that bond fade. Witnessing this pervasive tragedy, COL Cross committed to finding a mechanism for maintaining these relationships, regardless of the spatial divide. So, in a time when email was still a novelty, he used his annual Christmas letter to not only stay in contact with friends and family, but also as a means of touching base with his respected former leaders. As a result, throughout his career, he had the benefit of regular advice and support from several experienced senior leaders outside of his chain of command.

We talked a bit more on the subject, probing and asking questions, partly interested in the professional development opportunities, and partly trying to filibuster and avoid getting to real classwork. But eventually we'd stalled long enough and COL Cross sent us up to the boards to tackle some newly crafted physics problems. Still, as we navigated through various intellectual puzzles, I couldn't help but daydream about that night's festivities, as well as this newfound mentorship advice.

As class drew to a close, we packed up our books, thanked our teacher for another great class, and started making our way to our next class. But before I made it to the door, COL Cross called out to me.

"Stick around for a moment. I want to talk to you," he said, gesturing me over to his desk.

I was pretty sure I hadn't done anything wrong, and his tone was jovial, but anytime the teacher asks you to stay after class it can make you nervous.

"What's up, sir?" I asked, trying not to seem too anxious.

"You're not in trouble or anything," he added, assuaging the apparently obvious look of fear on my face. "Listen," he continued. "Your time at the academy is drawing to a close. You're a good student, motivated and engaged, and I wanted to let you know that I think you should consider returning as a teacher."

I almost laughed. With graduation so close, all I could think about was getting as far from West Point as possible. Now he wanted me to think about coming back. It was almost unthinkable. Again, reading my mind, he continued.

"It's years down the road, and you don't have to make a decision now, but I want you to stay open to it. Keep in contact and when the time comes, really think about it."

Flattered but unsure, I thanked him and promised to earnestly consider. As I turned to walk towards the door, COL Cross spoke again.

"Stay in touch. I'm always around if you have questions."

"Will do, sir!" I smiled and said with seriousness, and walked out.

Dinner that night was as amazing as any I had seen. The mess hall was extravagantly decorated in holiday memorabilia by the staff. Each year they build an elaborate gingerbread house in the middle of the hall. This year it was designed to be a miniature, cookie version of the cadet chapel. Plebes from around the corps competed to garnish their tables with outlandish and often huge festive adornments. Some had working model trains, another had a giant inflatable Santa, and someone even managed to chop down a humongous pine tree and erect it at their table, complete with lights and a glowing star at the top. Foolishness of the best kind!

Garbed in our finest full-dress uniforms, we passed around silly gifts, chugged down eggnog, and told fantastical stories about our time at the academy. Then, as is tradition, the dinner ended in song as we stood on our chairs singing "The Twelve Days of Christmas" before heading out onto the apron, a large concrete area in front of the mess hall, for the yearly cigar smoke. Standing outside on the apron, four thousand cadets gathered together in joyous comradery, sharing in the delicious stink of a fine Christmas cigar. Everyone was laughing and embracing, posing for pictures with friends and telling stories. There wasn't a care in the world. We all knew what lay only a few short months ahead; we would leave, we would deploy, we would fight. And, as reminded by the all too often moments of silence at meals, we also knew that some of us would not return. But for now, on this one night, the constant pressure that loomed over our heads seemed to wane as we celebrated our last Christmas together.

I wondered how many people outside our walls ever got to experience the joy of such a night. I was struck by how profoundly blessed I was to share in the moment. Knowing it was my last time, a mix of joy and sadness filling my chest and I stopped to soak in the moment, watching as clouds of white cigar smoke wafted into the cold winter air. Then, as I raised my eyes to the heavens, I noticed fat, soft flakes drifting down to the earth and smiled upwards as they greeted me on the cheek. My wish had come true, it was snowing!

Almost exactly one year later, miles away from my rock-bound-highland-home (aka West Point), I sat at my kitchen table watching as the last, determined leaves fell from the tree outside my window. They wafted down slowly, illuminated by the glow of the lights we had hung from our awning. North Carolina winters were much too mild for snowfall, but still, watching as the leaves fluttered to the ground, I found myself drawn back to that night surrounded by all my friends. They were gone now, scattered around the globe and sitting at their own kitchen tables, I presumed. Or maybe they were downrange fighting. I recalled the image of us swaying back and forth, signing carols at the top of our lungs.

Dear God, please let them be okay.

Were they happy and healthy, or were they struggling to get by? From the other room, I could hear my wife turning over in her sleep. It was late but I couldn't sleep. My heart was heavy thinking of my friends. I was so lucky to have someone; too many of our friends were alone. Again, I said I silent prayer that they were safe. Then, a forgotten memory reemerged; it was the conversation with COL Cross about Christmas letters. *How simple,* I thought, committing myself to write one the following day.

So, that next night, my wife and I sat down to craft our first Christmas letter as a family. We snuggled up beside the fire, hot cocoa in hand, and began recounting the various adventures of the previous year. When it was done, we printed out a copy, set it on the table, and stepped back to admire our work. The letter itself was fairly bland—white with a small trim of green holly around the boarder. But, looking down at the simple slip of paper, we couldn't help but swell with pride as we reviewed *our* letter, a symbol of our life together.

We sent it out to only a few people that first year—family, friends, old instructors, and of course … COL Cross. I made sure to write an additional note to him, thanking him for the idea. We also included our contact info at the bottom, encouraging people to reach back out and share their own stories. Almost immediately, I received an excited phone call from COL Cross wishing us happy tidings and gushing over how much we'd grown. We talked for at least an hour, sharing stories, discussing future plans, and telling him of various leadership challenges I was facing. In return, he provided encouragement and passed on sage wisdom born of his own experiences. Everything seemed so clear and effortless for him, it was amazing to listen as he so clearly got to the heart of any issue. In that short phone call, I might have received more golden nuggets of wisdom than I had managed to pick up throughout the previous six months.

To our joyful surprise, he wasn't the only one to reach out. We received an incredible outpouring of love and support from our friends around the globe. We spent the better part of a month reconnecting with people, each time rejoicing as old friendships burned bright again. How easily we had let them slip out of our life. But then again, how easily it was for them to slip back into our lives, seamlessly falling into the playful banter of old friends. We decided then to commit ourselves to reaching out at least once a year to keep the flame of friendship burning bright. It was also a great way to keep in contact with past leaders and mentors as an azimuth check. Like looking down to check your compass as you find your way through the wilderness, regular check-ins with such guides helps to ensure you're still on the right path.

Since that first year, the whole operation has grown substantially. Not only have my graphic design skills improved dramatically since that initial letter, but our list of friends and mentors continues to grow with each new duty station. However, though the style and scope of these letters have changed through the years, one constant has been the persistent and supportive presence of COL Cross and other beloved mentors. Upon receiving our letters, they call to share their own stories and provide wisdom and guidance. Throughout deployments, in the face of leadership challenges, when we've had especially frustrating bosses, or difficult career decisions, these mentors have shepherd us through some of the hardest crucibles and we've emerged all the better. During this special time of year, we honor this rare opportunity to reconnect and celebrate the great triumphs in each other's lives.

On our fifth year of this tradition, I added an extra note to COL Cross's letter. At the very bottom, I told him I'd be interested in talking to him about teaching. I was about halfway through my time as a company commander and needed to start looking at post-command options. Over the years, the visceral frustrations of being a cadet faded and as I looked back at our time at the academy, I couldn't help but feel the fondness and warmth of nostalgia. I expected his return message to be exuberant and forceful, like a fisherman eagerly reeling in their catch after finally getting a nibble. But that's not how it went down. Certainly, he was happy for me and acknowledged my sense of thawing on the matter. However, he never once pushed me in that direction. Instead, he listened. He let me lay out all my thoughts, list out my options, and go through a cost-benefit analysis. Meanwhile, he listened stoically, only interjecting to ask a pointed question or two before letting ramble onward lost in my thoughts.

After I'd expended myself, going through each and every detail of the seemingly endless list of my thoughts on the matter, I finally paused and turned the conversation to him.

"So, what should I do?" I finally asked.

There was a long intake of breath on the other side of the phone like he was thinking deeply about the question. A part of me, the still young and impatient part of me, hoped he would just come out and say, "that's easy, you should ..." But of course, he was too seasoned a teacher to go that route. Instead, he told me a story.

"Do you remember when I told you about how we write the Christmas letters every year?" he asked. "Well, there's more to it. Eventually, after enough years, you build up quite a collection. It's almost like a book about your life where each page holds a full year of your journey. Obviously more happens during that year than can fit onto the little page, but you get the highlights, the important stuff. So here you are, looking down at the most exciting story you'll ever read except, and here's the interesting part, you don't yet know how the story ends. But that doesn't mean you can't see where you're headed, what direction you're moving towards."

"I can't tell you want you should do," he continued. "At the end of the day, you've got to be the one to make the decision about what kind of life you want to lead. Pay attention to your story; after all, you are the main character. What's the next chapter in your book? Where do you want your story to lead? What needs to happen to get you from the path that you're on now all the way to that happy ending? For me, teaching was the most exciting and rewarding times of my life, both personally and professionally. Getting to make an impact on students like you has been one of my greatest joys. But there were sacrifices too. You've got to be the one to decide. I think you'd be a great fit as a teacher, but you've got to make the call."

That night, I gathered our little family around the fireplace and began the first installment of what has now grown to be our absolute favorite family Christmas tradition. Starting from the beginning, we read through each of our previous years' letters, reminiscing about all that has led to our current adventure. Amidst the chaos and turmoil of everyday life, it is an opportunity for us to stop and reflect on all the blessings we have enjoyed. Moreover, it's a chance to teach our children about the story of their history. Each year, they become ever more interested in hearing how their parents, young and in love, overcame challenges and moves and deployments, to come together to form the family we are today. It's a beautiful and cathartic ritual which we cherish to this day.

But that first time, all those years ago, served a special purpose. In addition to reminiscing about all the fun it has been building a life together, I also took note of what things I found most important. Each year, in almost every letter while talking about what I found most professionally fulfilling, I talked about how much I loved developing others. Whether it was helping a teammate cope with the challenges of back-to-back deployments or motivating new recruits as they progress through basic training, my great passion was always about helping others become a better version of themselves. Simultaneously, I realized that this was exactly what COL Cross and so many others did for me. They exemplified what I wanted to be. So that night, after putting our kids to bed, I hopped on the computer and submitted my application to return to West Point to teach.

We all need mentorship. It helps us to learn and grow, to listen to a wisdom born of experience and help guide us on our path. We need the connection and a set of fresh and trained eyes to inspect our problems. Too often we find ourselves in the crisis of the moment, fighting to survive and unable to see a clear way ahead. But by having a guide standing a safe distance from the problem, they have the space and experience to illuminate a safe path forward. Without such mentorship, we are lost, wondering through a jungle hoping to find our own way.

We all need help along our path. Think about Mary and Joseph along their journey to Bethlehem, hoping to find safety and shelter. Through the help of mentorship, we are able to take refuge along our journey as we rest, recuperate, and chart our path forward.

Equally as important as seeking out good mentorship is the act of finding a mentor. These are similar, but not the same thing. It is not enough to simply ask for advice from any passerby. So many young officers will just reach out to those around them, whatever leader happens to be within arm's reach at the time. And while you should absolutely leverage every available resource, forging new relationships wherever you go, you cannot develop such bonds solely out of proximity. Designate an individual, or individuals, whom you resonate with as a mentor. Seek out and formalize the bond as they help decode your life's stories and light your path ahead. By staying connected through the years, such a connection strengthens and matures, providing even greater benefits as you share in each other's stories.

On a cold and dark December evening, two years into my tour as an assistant professor at the academy, I trudged out to the mailbox to bring in the post. The early winter sunsets combined with the unyieldingly long workdays gave an illusion of eternal darkness. Even with all the decorations ornamenting the long row of identical Army housing duplexes, the cold blackness can start to wear you down. So, there I was, suffering the wind and the snow as part of the mindless daily routine, when I opened the latch to our box and a small red envelope fell into my hands. I rolled the letter around in my hand, wondering about the sender. There was no postmark which meant someone had made the trek to deliver it by hand. Suddenly, as realization struck me, the wind began quiet and the air grew warmer. It was a letter from a former student. Wanting to pass on the wisdom of COL Cross, I'd made a point throughout my few years in touting the benefits of the whole Christmas card experience. But, I was on the receiving end of this sacred tradition. You cannot imagine the incredible, overwhelming feelings of pride, gratitude, and humility you experience in a moment like that. It was the best Christmas gift.

You might not realize it yet, but you are at the beginning of a grand adventure. It might not always seem like it when intermixed with the banality of everyday life, but I promise something exhilarating is taking place. This life, *your* life, is a true gift from God. I think it is easy for us to forget that sometimes. Don't rush through, stop and pay attention. Imagine what a tragedy it would be to visit the Louvre and sprint through as fast as possible. Similarly, you must stop and soak in the magnificent beauty of the living art that is your life. Besides giving you a better appreciation for your story, your experiences can help you to learn and grow in ways you never imagined.

19 ···· NUMBER YOUR STORIES

"Child," said the lion, "I am telling you your story, not hers. No one is told any story but their own." – C.S. Lewis, The Horse and His Boy

I have been blessed with many amazing experiences throughout my military career. Every duty station has been filled with incredible friends, exciting adventures, and rewarding opportunities. I've traveled the globe and served in combat. I've jumped out of airplanes and welcomed thousands of new recruits into the Army ranks. But the best thing I've ever done in uniform was teach.

I have always had a proclivity for physics. Perhaps it's a bit nerdy, but I've long since come to terms with it. Thanks to an inspirational high school science teacher, Ms. Reisinger, I discovered a passion and talent for the subject. There is something about learning to understand the order and beauty in the design of our universe that resonated with me on a deep level. It was Ms. Reisinger who recognized this passion and encouraged me to pursue this yet untapped potential. At her prodding, I attended the regional physics competition—yes, there are physics competitions—after one of the other participants dropped out at the last minute. I'll never forget showing up on the first day wearing my usual letterman jacket attire, only to be chided by the other kids for being a "dumb jock." But Ms. Reisinger saw past all of that and helped me find my way, which eventually led to my winning the competition. I was hooked.

Sustaining this affinity throughout my college years at West Point, I decided to major in physics. Again, my passion for the subject continued to grow. This, however, seemed to be a relatively unique response in comparison to my classmates. As a core class, all students were forced to take it, regardless of their interest. The notoriously difficult subject had a reputation for lengthy and challenging homework. Wanting to help my friends and classmates, I started tutoring on a regular basis. Gathered with my friends, as we huddled around a whiteboard solving problems, I found the experience tremendously exciting. Eventually, I learned that what I enjoyed even more than learning physics, was *teaching* physics.

Over the following decade, I stayed in relatively close contact with my mentors in the department, as I do to COL Cross. With time—and a bit of luck—I eventually was fortunate to have the opportunity to return as an instructor, and it was an absolute dream come true. In the decade apart from my beloved "House of PaNE" (Physics and Nuclear Engineering), I had developed this idyllic (almost utopian) image of the life of an instructor. But none of these fantasies compared with the true richness and fulfillment that came from working with the cadets daily.

You see, I had—quite mistakenly—believed my chief purpose was centered in the mere teaching of physics. After all, I was hired as a physics instructor; it all seemed rather self-explanatory. But this was a gross mischaracterization. Certainly, physics was involved, but this was simply a mechanism—no, an *excuse*—for us to discuss deeper concepts like leadership and character.

It might shock you to learn that not everyone is enthusiastic about the prospect of taking physics. In fact, many of the students show up on the first day of class with wildly negative preconceptions. If it weren't so sad, it could almost be comical to see them all prior to the start of class—sweaty and nervous. The better part of the semester is spent coaxing them out of hiding to forge a bond of trust and respect. No, we are not here to *get you*. Yes, I want you to be successful. Sometimes it is a struggle, but it always pays off in the end.

Every single day, in every single class, I felt that I had an opportunity to make an impact on someone's life. I saw examples of this in the struggling student who finally had everything *click* after weeks of hard work, the energetic pupil who became excited about solving a puzzle for the first time in their academic career, and the late-night phone call of a lost soul—frightened and alone—as they reach out for someone they trust in a time of need. All of these cadets brought vibrancy and purpose to my life. It is truly humbling to think I had the privilege of participating in the journey of these young leaders; leaders who will surely go on to surpass my own level of ability.

As if they are my own flesh and blood—my brothers and sisters—I have grown to love them. And like family, they make me laugh, get upset, and occasionally want to pull my hair out; and yet, I still love them. Each day I thanked the Lord for that sincerely rewarding opportunity. It filled me with joy and amazement that such poetry and emotion can take root in a field of study thought by many to be cold and overly scientific. How ironic.

I think that most students showed up on their first day expecting to confront boring problems pulled form dusty chalk-covered old books. But somehow, amidst all the equations and numbers, they saw beyond that. They began to uncover the hidden artistry of the universe, elegant and perfectly woven. They were curious and creative, seeking out truth as they asked probing questions and challenged their existing theories. They pushed the boundaries of their knowledge and embraced the unknown. Like explorers, we sought to explain and demystify the physical world while acknowledging our limitations. They asked "why," pushing their way forward to the very edge of what we understand and stared into the great unknown. Just like Columbus or Magellan, maybe *you* will be the one to press onward and uncover something new.

The greatest joys blossomed out of the human interactions behind all the science. Cheering on a challenged student as they wrestled with a difficult problem and seeing the spark of delight and recognition in their eyes as they finally understood the solution; pushing a talented student to delve further and find a yet uncovered "sprankle" of science-y goodness; encouraging a timid and unsure student to become comfortable speaking—these were the sorts of things that truly made teaching worthwhile. The more I focused on these extra-curriculars, the greater impact I began to experience. So, I began to search for new ways to approach these moments.

Midway through my first semester, I observed a technique I found most intriguing. In the hopes of improving my skillset as an instructor and mentor, I frequently sat in on a variety of other classes from around the institution. Of course, I watched other science programs and found them helpful. But the most enlightening experiences were from my visits to those subjects most different than my own, such as writing composition, English literature, and history. Though greatly different than my own discipline, I was confronted with the most unique and often beneficial ideas. Without hesitation, I began shamelessly stealing such techniques for my own pedagogical toolkit.

One of these ideas was to name my chalkboards. Each board title should correspond with some enlightening personal experience throughout my career. At the end of each lesson, assuming the class had gone well, I would let the students pick one of these personal stories. I would then spend the remaining few minutes sharing the tale and discussing my lessons learned from the experience. Ironically, out of all the topics covered, from Newton's Laws through conservation of momentum, the most frequent comment I receive from students is about how much they remembered these stories. Still, I generally regarded them as a mere fun activity to end class. It wasn't until the retirement of a close mentor that I began to understand the possibility for my "little stories."

COL Edward Naessens, later promoted to Brigadier General, holds a special place in my heart. As my instructor, mentor, and department head, his leadership and wisdom has been a touchstone throughout my career. Like thousands of others, I found my life forever transformed by his example of humble servant leadership. So, when it came time for him to retire, word spread like wildfire. With over thirty-seven years of service to our nation, this great man walked into his classroom to teach his last physics lesson at West Point. As a testament to the lives forever changed by his example, nearly a hundred people from around the globe traveled to attend in person or observed virtually. And even more sent letters and well wishes.

As I sat in the large classroom, surrounded by former students—both young and old—the warm and comforting feeling of nostalgia permeated through the air. With the poise and grace of an experienced educator, COL Naessens effortlessly traversed the lesson material, engaging and inspiring every student. But as the lesson drew to a close, he pivoted. It is common for a teacher to use the last minutes of class to transition to some broader life lesson, but this seemed to have the grave and purposeful tone of a man in the twilight of his career.

He told a few stories and, as always, provided tremendously sound guidance. But as he concluded, he looked beyond his normal class towards those of us filling the back of the room and gave a final parting word of advice: number your stories. He went on to explain that any good leader, or at least anyone who is paying attention, is graced with a plethora of rich and meaningful stories. Some are funny, others somber, but these stories dot the landscape of our memory as we reflect upon our experiences. In the retelling of these anecdotes, we remember and respect our past as we share our lessons learned with future leaders. This is sacred and wonderful, but there can be even more discovered from our stories. It is one thing to amass a wealth of go-to anecdotes but by formalizing each story, naming and creating an order for how they are told, and examining the purpose and lesson of each, you can learn a tremendous amount about yourself.

To "number your stories" is to transform a seemingly random collection of interesting events into a formalized and coherent narrative of your journey on this earth. In COL Naessens' words, the act of numbering your stories can illuminate a deeper, unforeseen plotline of your life. Do not merely write down your stories but try to comprehend their role in your development as a person and visualize how each tale ties to the rest. Form narrative groupings unbound by the limits of chronology and bestow your own order and sequence. Through this act, you can step back from the crisis of everyday moments to see a larger picture. Think of the historic wartime commanders: each lieutenant on the battlefield understands their assigned mission with grave detail, but it is the general atop the hill who sees the entirety of the conflict and can understand how each battle shapes the war.

Imagine you are standing too closely to your television screen.[6] Instead of your regularly scheduled program, you see a bunch of flickering red, blue and green dots. Discrete and seemingly independent, these pixels appear unconnected from the rest as they turn on and off with apparent randomness. But when you take a step back, allowing the space to think and breathe, you see how each piece is just a small part of a larger and more beautiful picture. In this same way, the process of numbering your stories can give shape and meaning to your life by revealing a narrative previously unknown. At least, that is what COL Naessens seemed to

---

[6] I'm not sure why, but my kids love to do this.

believe. And on the last day of this great man's career in the military, out of everything he could have chosen, this was the lesson he decided to share.

So, I took it to heart and committed myself to the challenge. I opted to not only number my stories but decided that I was going to write them down. Over the subsequent three years, filled with numerous late nights and a multitude of drafts and edits, I would learn that this task was decidedly *not* easy. Certainly, I had the stories, but it was the act of putting them onto paper that I found taxing beyond belief. In all sincerity, I must have written and deleted this book at least five times. As someone who considered themselves an accomplished storyteller, it seemed so frustrating to struggle so much with putting words on the page. But you see, when you tell a story in person, it is like a flame—fluid and always moving. You can adjust the emphasis or embellish portions of the tale, depending on who is listening. If they do not understand a part, you can elaborate. If they seem bored, you speed up. With each new telling, there are endless possibilities. But when you commit the story to paper, you freeze it in time forever. What is on the page exists, and everything else is lost. What a tremendous amount of pressure![7]

Nevertheless, I persisted in the endeavor and discovered the rich truth about what COL Naessens had prescribed. Though frustrating, I can say with certainty that the ritual of selecting, analyzing, and ordering each of these personal parables has been an intensely cathartic, and often spiritual experience. Forcing myself to manifest my thoughts and feelings onto the page, crystalizing them from abstraction into reality, has sharpened and magnified my own understanding of the journey I've been walking.

Throughout my life, often there would be events that felt profound, and I filed the experience away in my mind to revisit at a later date. But that time never came, or at least not as quickly as it should. Instead, those

---

[7] If anything, this experience has granted me with a healthy dose of humility and a great deal of respect for my brothers and sisters in the humanities. My hat is off to you!

memories and emotions, lessons to be learned, sat untouched for years in dusty old boxes in some forgotten corner of my mind. Well, that was until I began this endeavor.

But once I started to unpack those boxes, revisiting old memories and seeing them with a new eye, I was amazed at the hidden treasures that had sat untended for so long. For the most part, time and distance had largely freed me from any emotional chains which had barred me from seeing the full picture in the midst of the event. And any remaining attachments were severed through the mechanics of analyzing, ordering and editing. Somewhere in the middle of all that procedure, I felt the last little thread snap from within and any negative emotions surrounding the memories just floated away.

It was like I was revisiting stories from a movie I had seen before. I knew the plot, but wasn't overly emotionally invested, almost as if they were about someone else. And in a sense, that was true. Those things might have happened to the younger me, but that wasn't me anymore. I was older and wiser. I can look back with gratitude at that younger me for having survived so many adventures. After all, I wouldn't be where I am today without that young chucklehead.

Watching these "memory movies," without the burden of emotional attachment, allows you to finally process them. You can watch anew with a critical eye and at long last squeeze the juice from their fruit. I've always liked the movie "Memento," but if you've never seen it, think of a mystery thriller with a great twist at the end. Watching it for the first time is epic and awesome, as you experience all the excitement. But it's almost just as fun to watch it again for a second (or tenth) time, uncovering all the things you had missed before. Now that you know the ending, you can truly appreciate the fuller context of the rest of the movie. You understand why characters are acting in peculiar ways and the hidden significance of events, which at first seemed benign.

The same is true for your own stories. When looking back, you can start to see themes and connections that perhaps you didn't before. Does one story impact another? Are you relearning the same lesson in multiple stories? For example, it was not until I began this book that I realized the connection between the shark-eyed boys, my career in bodybuilding, and the ultimate destruction of my pectoral muscle. Throughout all this, God was teaching me, using my own actions and their consequences to show me something important.

Lastly, I'll point out that this process has significantly helped me to formalize my thoughts and opinions on various issues. Just as the act of formalizing the stories onto the page proved challenging, so was the act of crystalizing my opinions on leadership issues. Obviously, I've always had a general sense of what was important and can comfortably share various ideas to address leadership challenges of mentees. But those things exist in a milieu; a mist that is fluid and changing. Forcing myself to pick out, specifically, what is important enough to share was tough, but rewarding. This act is something which I thoroughly advocate to anyone wanting to gain a fuller appreciation for their life as they develop as a leader.

Now, you don't have to write a whole book. But take some time each week, maybe just an hour, to sit and reflect on the things that have happened in your life. Give yourself space to think and breath. What was the lesson? What did you learn? How do you grow? Keep a journal to jot down any themes or golden nuggets. If you are super "hooah," get yourself one of those official Army green leader books so it feels extra official.

"But I don't have any stories," you might be saying. Wrong. In fact, it's the exact opposite. The truth is that you have so many stories that each one of them is getting lost among the rest, but to become a great storyteller, you need to first become an avid collector of stories. Take a moment to think about your day. Was there a moment that emotionally moved you? Were you upset with your boss? Maybe you had a powerful interaction with a struggling soldier who needed your help? Did you supremely screw something up and narrowly escape shame and disaster?

These are your stories, filled with golden nuggets ripe for the pickin! Jot down a brief outline, just the five W's and how you felt. Before long, you'll have a huge library. Then, go back and read the story of your life, and give yourself time to celebrate it. Understand where you've come from and where you are going. Find someone to stand beside you as you embrace the challenging moments together and drive towards the most sacred parts of existence. Remain connected and seek out guidance and mentorship as you interpret the lessons of your age. And, as you go through life, take time to stop and give thanks for this great gift God has given you.

Remember, you were made for a reason. Pay attention to the deeper narrative being revealed to you and learn. Constantly push yourself to grow. But most of all, respect your life and number your stories.

···· KINDLE THE FLAME

"I hope I didn't bore you too much with my life's story." - Elvis
Presley

The night is growing colder and the fire is dying down. The few tongues
of flame sputter and lick up at the sky as the last remaining fragments of
wood relinquish their final stores of energy. Their brittle remains crumble
to ash amidst the lingering red backdrop of warm, crackling coals. In the
distance, you can hear the quite chirp of crickets singing into the crisp
night air and the rustle of small furry animals as they scurry about in the
darkness just beyond the waning glow of our once-fire. Our evening
together is drawing to a close. My glass is dry and it is time to go.

But rest assured, this will not be the last of such an evening. Many,
many more lay ahead for you, whether back at this fire, returning as an
eager pupil or maybe around your own hearth, recounting your own tales
to the next generation. Like the fire before us, this chapter of my story is
drawing to a close, glowing embers dimming in the night. I look back on

this portion of my life with joy and gratitude as I prepare for what lies ahead, hopefully wiser from that which I've left behind. However, your own story is just beginning. Your flame hopefully kindled even more by my own, just as my predecessors passed on their light to me. Through the ages we continue to pass on the blaze, from one generation to the next, burning bright within the chest of those who answer the call. I am deeply honored and humbled to have gotten the chance to share my stories with you. Thank you for the opportunity. Now, as you begin your own adventure, recall the lessons learned here this night.

Firstly, uncover the strength of a winning team by clearly discovering and articulating a shared purpose. Rally about this calling, providing a home for those in our charge grounded in shared values. Provide your team with an opportunity to excel. Push them towards greatness with compassionate discipline and allow them to reach their potential and earn their place. Amidst the hardship and challenges that surely lay ahead, band together and celebrate the bonds of philia and the assurance that you have their back.

Secondly, reflect on your past and identify those events that are preventing you from advancing on your journey. Like an anchor weighing you down, find a way to sever the tie to those things that keep you from moving forward. Remember, you have been created by God for something special. Listen to His voice as you look within to find your strength and push forward in a constant pursuit of unattainable perfection. Set outrageous goals and move towards them one step at a time, growing ever closer to the person you were meant to be. And above all, rise above your past as you strive for greatness, not for the glory, but because the act of striving is righteous.

Thirdly, continue to grow as a professional to consistently achieve excellent results. Look beyond the superficial, earnestly digging through your experience to find the hidden gold nuggets of success. Often, the most beneficial lessons are complex, intricate systems which require a granular, deft touch. Listen to others and analyze their progression such that you may learn from their path. But ultimately, you must find your own way. Don't waste time trying to transform into someone else, rather, become the best version of yourself.

Lastly, as you fly through your career, flawlessly knocking down targets as they zip past, don't forget to take a moment to reflect. Understand where your story fits into the bigger picture. Only by knowing where you've come from can you determine which way you are going. As you walk this path forward, find a partner to share in the struggles and victories alongside you. Cherish the moments, both good and bad, as they each form the dense and beautiful tapestry of life. Even the hard times often lead to the most special of moments. As you navigate through the wilderness, find a mentor to help guide you through the unknown. Respect and learn from the life you've been gifted as you enjoy your adventure and number your stories.

Again, thank you for taking the time to listen to my stories as you begin your own adventure. When you have the time, I strongly encourage you to put pen to paper and compose your own narrative. By jotting down some thoughts, you'll significantly develop as a professional.

Though confined to our imagination, across the bounds of space and time, I have thoroughly enjoyed our evening together. In all sincerity and seriousness, as you begin your journey and head out to make your mark on the world, I would cherish any opportunity to listen to your stories or provide guidance.

You can reach me at *logan.phillips.author@gmail.com*.

May God bless you and America,
Logan J. Phillips

.... ABOUT THE AUTHOR

Logan Phillips is a career Army officer, former Basic Training Commander, Assistant Professor of Physics at the United States Military Academy (USMA) at West Point, and author of *Number Your Stories and Lead Like a Legend*. Having spent over a decade shaping the next generation of military leaders, Logan remains passionate about inspiring others to meet their potential. Logan is also a nuclear physicist with degrees from USMA and Yale University, and winner of the 2021 "Dean's Teaching Excellence Award." His work is hailed by former superintendent, LTG (R) Robert Caelen as "the blueprint for leadership that achieves success and significance."

During his free-time, Logan coaches his boys' football team and writes children's literature. His acclaimed children's book *I Love You More* released in 2021, and all proceeds are donated to support Gold-Star Children.